IF I REALLY WANTED TO
GROW CLOSER TO GOD,
I WOULD . . .

Honor Books
Tulsa, Oklahoma

If I Really Wanted to Grow Closer to God, I Would . . .
ISBN 1-56292-567-9
Copyright © 2000 by Honor Books
P.O. Box 55388
Tulsa, Oklahoma 74155

Manuscript prepared by Hafer & Associates,
Colorado Springs, Colorado.

Introduction

Are you longing to grow closer to your Creator and gain understanding concerning His great love for you and His purpose for your life? If so, then this book was written for you.

The journey to knowing God is a personal one. However, this book has been designed to provide simple tips and insights to help you on your way. Can we guarantee that you will find what you are looking for? Of course not, but God can. The Bible encourages the true seeker to "Come near to God and he will come near to you" (James 4:8). If you are truly searching for Him with an open heart, you will find what you are looking for.

May God bless you as you embark upon and endeavor to renew your spiritual journey.

Grow Closer to God,

I Would . . .

Be on the lookout for miracles.

*The whole crowd of disciples
began joyfully to praise God
in loud voices for all the
miracles they had seen.*
—Luke 19:37

Does God part seas anymore? Or feed people with manna from heaven? Maybe you haven't witnessed a miracle of biblical proportions recently. But then again, maybe you haven't had your eyes open wide enough to see both the spectacular and the simple, but amazing, acts of God right in front of you.

You already know this first-hand, don't you. After all, isn't it a miracle when a person's life—when your life—is changed because of a brand-new response to God's love?

So open your eyes and heart to God's miracles. Expect them, want them, and enjoy them when they occur. *When.* Not *if.* Because as you grow closer to God, your life will be nothing short of miraculous.

❧

Miracles tend to happen to those whose eyes are open to see them.

Grow Closer to God,

I Would . . .

Strive for a
personal relationship
with Him.

*That is His call to us—simply to
be people who are content to live
close to Him and to renew the
kind of life in which the
closeness is felt and experienced.*
—Thomas Merton

There is a big difference between knowing *about* God and truly knowing Him personally and directly. Take time to be still in God's presence, and ask Him to fill your head and your heart with His love and wisdom. Books, sermons, and music can all help you experience God's presence, but they should only be pathways to God, not destinations unto themselves.

You can't read a movie review, for example, and get the same experience as seeing the movie yourself. And you can't truly understand someplace on the globe by pouring over a travel brochure. You must go to the place and enjoy it firsthand.

*Your relationship with God is one thing
you should take personally.*

Admit when I'm wrong.

*If we confess our sins,
he is faithful and just and will
forgive us our sins and purify us
from all unrighteousness.*
—1 John 1:9

No one likes to admit doing wrong. And yet, when we confess our mistakes to God and to those we have hurt or offended, we are, in a sense, admitting that we are not perfect and that we need God's grace in our lives. It is a sad person who insists that he or she has no need of God's grace. Such a person will never know the sweet comfort of collapsing into God's arms and hearing Him say, "I forgive you."

Don't let pride and denial limit your possibilities. God is wise and good. Clear away all that might keep you from knowing Him fully.

There is no plea bargaining with God.

Set my "pet grudge" free.

*Therefore, rid yourselves
of all malice.*
—1 Peter 2:1

Maybe that "pet grudge" was cute when you first got it. But not anymore. It has grown big and demanding and ugly. Its whining and complaining annoy you and those around you. And it keeps leaving those unsightly stains on your soul. So, it's time to set the grudge free. After all, God says that we must not be resentful (2 Timothy 2:24).

Open your heart's door and shoo the grudge away. Then forgive the person who gave it to you in the first place. You will feel better. Your heart will feel lighter. And if that grudge ever comes back and scratches at your door, pretend you're not home.

Those who hold grudges aren't able to hold on to God—or much of anything else.

Grow Closer to God,

I Would . . .

Exercise my right to write in my Bible.

✿

*If you are serious about your
faith, put it in writing.*
—Taylor Morgan

Reading the Bible should be an interactive experience. As you read, think about how to apply God's words to your life. Write down action steps you plan to take. Underline passages you want to memorize. Highlight portions you are confused about and remind yourself to ask someone about them. The power of God's words does not reside in the impressive leather binding or the gilded edges of the pages, but in their ability to sink into your thoughts and soul.

If you still feel awkward about marking up your Bible, buy a notebook and use it to chronicle your thoughts and responses to God's life instruction manual and personal love letter.

To get the most out of studying the Bible, you need the write stuff!

Grow Closer to God,

I Would . . .

Avoid being a pew potato.

It's great to have your feet on the ground, but keep them moving.

—American Proverb

Are you a pew potato? A religious russet? A spiritual spud? Do you merely sit in church week after week, letting the messages and music slide through your ears without making an impression on your brain or your heart?

If so, it's time for a change. Actively *listen* to your pastor's words. Think about how you can apply them to your life—immediately. If the pastor brings up a wrong you are struggling with, ask for forgiveness right away. If you are reminded of the struggles of a family member or friend, make a note to pray for that person or write a letter of encouragement. The point is: do something, anything. Don't just sit there, get spiritually active.

*Being a pew potato leads to
a half-baked spiritual life.*

Grow Closer to God,

I Would . . .

Pray the Lord's Prayer every day.

❧

Our Father in heaven, hallowed be your name, your kingdom come, your will be done on earth as it is in heaven. Give us today our daily bread. Forgive us our debts, as we also have forgiven our debtors. And lead us not into temptation, but deliver us from the evil one.

—Matthew 6:9-13

So great is God's love for us that He even taught us what to pray. So on those days you're not sure what to say to your Father, open up your Bible and follow Jesus' model. Better yet, memorize this prayer (if you haven't already).

Be careful though that you don't let the words become rote, ritualized, and meaningless. After every few words you pray, think about what they mean. Ask yourself, "Did I truly mean what I just said?" If the answer is "no," pray the words again. Another way to keep the Lord's Prayer fresh and vibrant in your life is to read or memorize it in several different Bible versions.

Make the Lord's Prayer your prayer as well.

Grow Closer to God,

I Would . . .

Hold a baby
in my arms.

*God's gifts put man's
best dreams to shame.*
—Elizabeth Barrett Browning

When people think of God, they tend to think of the Red Sea-parting, earthquake-making God. And awesome power is certainly part of who He is. But God also revealed Himself in the form of a helpless baby born in a manger 2,000 years ago. So the next time you hold a baby in your arms, imagine the Ruler of the Universe crying in hunger or shivering from the cold.

God could have come to earth as a full-grown, powerful man or a super-human hero. But He deliberately chose a harder, more humble road—a road that would be like the one we walk. Thus, He knows our experiences, our emotions, our humanity.

Thanks to God's great love, we need never say, "But you don't know what it's like down here."

Practice more walk, less talk.

*Go unto all the world
and preach the Gospel.
Use words if necessary.*
—St. Francis

A recent newspaper feature told of an episode of "road rage." The driver of a compact car cut in front of a pickup truck during rush hour. The pickup driver honked at the compact and hollered a few angry words. The other driver screamed back, made an obscene gesture, and sped away. The noteworthy part of this story is that the compact car was tattooed with Christian bumper stickers, including one that read, "WHAT WOULD JESUS DO?"

It's one thing to talk about how you are drawing closer to God or proclaim it with stickers and posters. It's another matter to live as God would want you to, even in the heat of rush hour.

A good example is the best sermon.

Grow Closer to God,

I Would . . .

Be proud
of Him.

⟨❧⟩

*Whoever acknowledges me before
men, I will also acknowledge
him before my Father in heaven.
But whoever disowns me before
men, I will disown him
before my Father in heaven.*
—Matthew 10:32,33

We are proud of our children, our yards, our cars, our achievements. We are eager to display them to others and to extol their many fine qualities. But it's sometimes a different story with God. We are afraid to identify ourselves as His children because we fear we will be criticized—or labeled as religious fanatics.

The next time you feel a sense of embarrassment over your desire to grow closer to God, ask yourself, "What do I have to be ashamed of?" After all, God is creative and powerful. He is loving. He is merciful. He is the perfect Father, and His children should be the proudest offspring in the world.

&

You can't be close to Him on the inside if you are afraid to acknowledge Him on the outside.

Practice patience.

One moment of patience may ward off great disaster.
—Chinese Proverb

Patience is part of God's character. If you want to grow closer to Him, you must cultivate and nourish it in your life. So the next time you're stuck in traffic or in a long, slow moving supermarket line, say to yourself, "I'm not going to let this situation get to me. I'm going to practice patience." Then use the time to pray for someone—how about the person testing your patience, for example?

Practicing patience with people and situations will help you better appreciate how patient God is with your own imperfections and mistakes. It will cause you to feel close to Him.

A handful of patience is better than a bucketful of brains.

Grow Closer to God,

I Would . . .

Put away
the Superman
(or Superwoman)
cape.

*The men who really believe
in themselves are all
in lunatic asylums.*
—G. K. Chesterton

Have you noticed how none of the TV or comic-book superheroes ever pray or go to church? Perhaps these individuals feel they don't need God. For us mortals, however, it's a different story. When you try to be a superhero and tackle life with your own human powers, you weaken your relationship with God.

Why? Because only when you admit you are weak can you experience His strength. Only when you acknowledge that you are sick can you know His healing. Only when you realize that you need His help, can you receive the help you need. So put your spirit of independence aside, and let Him meet your need.

🌿

Put away that superhero cape.
It doesn't go with what you're wearing.

Grow Closer to God,

I Would . . .

Determine to respect and obey God's rules of right living.

*I have hidden your word
in my heart that I might
not sin against you.*
—Psalm 119:11

Farmers have a saying that goes, "Once you're standing in the pig pen, it's too late to worry about soiling your Sunday clothes." And that advice carries beyond the farm. How can you grow close to God if you are busy doing those things that hurt Him, hurt you, and hurt others?

God has given us a code of conduct to live by. In the same way you would steer your child away from danger, these injunctions to right living are intended to steer you out of harm's way. Determine right now to resist those things that are contrary to God's rules of right living, and commit to avoid settings in which you'll likely face temptation.

An ounce of prevention is worth a pound of purity.

Honor my spouse.

*Successful marriage
is always a triangle:
a man, a woman, and God.*
—Cecil Myers

God could have used any number of analogies to illustrate His relationship with His followers: employer/employee, teacher/student, even master/slave. But the one He chose was groom/bride. Clearly, the relationship between husband and wife is important to Him.

So, when you praise, compliment, care for, and celebrate your spouse, you are honoring a relationship God Himself created—and you understand better how much God cherishes those who respond to His love and care. If you are single, the Bible says that God Himself will look after you as a husband. Direct your praises His way, and you will be, of all, the most blessed.

Divorce yourself from anything that comes between you and your spouse.

Grow Closer to God,

I Would . . .

Discover God's purpose for my life.

❦

*The purposes of the Almighty
are perfect, and must prevail,
though we erring mortals
may fail to accurately
perceive them in advance.*
—Abraham Lincoln

Do you have a sense of wonder about what you do in life? For example, if you're a teacher, are you merely downloading a bunch of facts upon your students or inspiring them with the thrill of learning? Is teaching just a job or is it a calling?

If what you do is just a job, you may have missed God's purpose for your life. Think of the first disciples Jesus called. They left all that they had to follow Him. Their hearts pounded with anticipation. Yours should as well. God's plan is for you to experience an abundant, vibrant life in perfect harmony with the gifts and callings He has placed in you. Find those and you will be one step closer to Him.

❧

Happiness is knowing what you were meant to be.

Practice humility.

The fear of the LORD teaches a man wisdom, and humility comes before honor.
—Proverbs 15:33

We live in a day in which those with political clout, wealth, beauty, and fame occupy the "Most Admired" lists. God's standards are different. Think of Jesus' parables. The last shall be first, and the first last. A small seed becomes a great tree. One lost sheep takes priority over the rest of the flock.

The Bible defines faith as walking humbly before God. And as we walk this way, practicing humility, we become more in tune with the character of a God who left heaven to become a vulnerable human. Someone who was so humble that He even made Himself subject to a humiliating and painful death—for our sake.

Those who sing their own praises usually sing solo.

Grow Closer to God,

I Would . . .

Remember
that He
is always
with me.

Where love is, there is God also.
—Leo Tolstoy

God cannot be contained in a building or a book. Yet we somehow forget Him unless we are in church or reading the Bible. Sometimes, in the midst of life's daily "busyness," we stop communicating with Him. Instead, our attention is on our computer screen, our checkbook, or the cars ahead of us in the traffic jam.

Don't allow life's details to turn your attention from your Creator. In the midst of your labor and duties, come to recognize that God is always right there with you—to hear you and to speak to you. His temple is always as close as your heart, waiting for you to enter and be refreshed and inspired.

~ॐ~

God is always just a prayer away.

Grow Closer to God,

I Would . . .

Rest.

Even the best racehorse
has to stop for oats
once in awhile.

—T. J. Bower

God doesn't sweat. He doesn't get tired. He doesn't struggle with aching muscles after a day of hard work. Yet the Bible says that when He finished creating the world, He rested. If our all-powerful God took the time to rest, that should speak volumes to us mere mortals.

You need to rest occasionally. You need to recover physically, emotionally, and spiritually from life's demands. And in resting, you will find the time and the right frame of mind to contemplate God's wonders and to thank Him for His grace and kindness to you. You will also gather the energy to run the next miles on your journey with Him, and toward Him.

To maintain good reception, you must keep your batteries charged.

Work on
my defense.

*Always be prepared to give
an answer to everyone who asks
you to give the reason for
the hope that you have.*
—1 Peter 3:15

If you were called into court and asked to defend God's existence and purpose, could you do it? Could you craft a compelling case to support your beliefs?

The Bible tells us to be ready to give a thoughtful, reasonable defense for the hope that is in us. So if you want to be closer to God, it's important to know why you believe that He exists at all and be able to support it intellectually. In the process of building a strong defense for your faith, you'll become more confident in your heart and mind that God does exist and wants to be personally involved in your life.

It doesn't matter what you believe until you know why you believe it.

Grow Closer to God,

I Would . . .

Give to those in need.

Do all the good you can,
By all the means you can,
In all the ways you can,
In all the places you can,
At all the times you can,
To all the people you can,
As long as ever you can.

—John Wesley

In one of His most compelling messages, Jesus taught that when we help the sick, the poor, the imprisoned, we help Him. He didn't say that it's *like* we're helping Him. He said, "I tell you the truth, whatever you did for one of the least of these brothers of mine, you did for me" (Matthew 25:40).

Thus, you must see Jesus in the hungry faces of third world children, the hopeless eyes of the street beggar, even the hardened expression of the convict. And as you see and give to Jesus by giving to those in need, you will be better able to appreciate all that He has given to you.

You can never outgive God.

Grow Closer to God,

I Would . . .

Explore the Christian classics.

*Christian literature
has some best sellers, but
even more blessed sellers.*
—Taylor Morgan

Want to be a good parent? Watch and learn from parents who are raising fulfilled, happy children. Want to be a good coach? Find one with a winning record and a team that respects him or her and competes with skill, maturity, and class.

But what about improving your spiritual life? Drawing closer to God? One way to accomplish this goal is to read the Christian classics. People like George MacDonald, C. S. Lewis, Martin Luther, and Charles Sheldon have honestly and eloquently written about many areas of Christian life and the challenges of growing closer to God. Their wisdom and inspiration are only a trip to the bookstore away.

Feed your mind and spirit: Read the classics.

Grow Closer to God,

I Would . . .

Remember
to say
"Thank you!"

❧

*Thanks be to God for his
indescribable gift!*
—2 Corinthians 9:15

Thanksgiving Day has been set aside as a time to thank God for our blessings. But if you are serious about growing closer to God, you shouldn't wait until you are gnawing on a turkey leg or stuffing yourself with dressing to thank God for all He has done.

Whenever you feel God's hand on your life, let Him know. When you see Him working in the lives of those around you, thank Him for that too. And don't worry if you're sometimes unsure how to express your deep gratitude for His goodness. Just thank Him the best way you can. He'll get the message. After all, He's God.

Gratitude is the key to happiness!

Grow Closer to God,

I Would . . .

Laugh more.

❧

*I believe God loves to
hear His children laugh.
What healthy father doesn't?*
—Mark Lowry

If you are a parent, uncle or aunt, teacher, baby-sitter, or coach, you know the pure joy that comes from hearing a child's laughter—especially if you had something to do with inspiring it. God invented laughter in order to nourish our souls. The Bible even records people using humor. Remember Elijah satirically taunting the prophets of Baal? Or Jesus' memorable words, "You strain out a gnat and swallow a camel"?

God always intended for us to enjoy His gift of laughter. So the next time you hear a funny story from the pulpit, a joke, or humorous song, don't rein in your laughter. Unleash it. Chances are, God is smiling, or even laughing right along with you.

Laughter is good medicine, and it's available without a prescription.

Grow Closer to God,

I Would . . .

Love my
enemies.

*You have heard that it was said,
"Love your neighbor and hate
your enemy." But I tell you:
Love your enemies and pray
for those who persecute you.*
—Matthew 5:43, 44

Is there any tougher commandment than the one to love our enemies? Not tolerate them or simply do kind things for them. Love them. Those obnoxious, cruel, hateful people—yeah, right!

The first step to loving your enemies is praying for them (not for their humiliation or destruction, by the way). And when you pray for your enemies, pray as much for your own attitudes and behaviors as for theirs. That way, even if your prayers don't change your enemies' ugly qualities, they will change yours. And as you experience what hard work it is to love unlovable people, you will value God's love more than ever.

Enemies are made, not born.

Approach someone unapproachable.

*They say, "Here is a glutton
and a drunkard, a friend of
tax collectors and 'sinners.'"
But wisdom is proved
right by her actions.*
—Matthew 11:19

In Jesus' time, Jews were legally forbidden to associate with the likes of beggars, tax collectors, and prostitutes. So when He befriended such people, Jesus didn't merely smash social and cultural barriers, He broke the law. And He didn't just spout Scriptures to these people. He ate with them. He touched them.

That's why it's so important for you to remember that the street beggars, drunks, and derelicts you encounter are loved by God as much as you are. And how you respond to them, how you treat them, is the true measure of your relationship with the heavenly Father.

What we do for the downtrodden, the outcasts we encounter, is what we do for Jesus.

Grow Closer to God,

I Would . . .

Slow down
to pray.

*If you haven't got the
time to talk to God,
you don't have a prayer.*
—Olivia Kent

Are your prayers quick monologues *to* God or conversations *with* God? Prayer is as much about listening to Him as it is speaking to Him. Often, we hit God with a barrage of requests, utter a few halfhearted "thank you's," then hurry on to the next order of the day. That is not prayer.

True prayer is unhurried. It's communication with your heavenly Father, the Creator of the universe. So slow down. Enter His presence in quietness and reverence. Pay attention to the words and feelings you get from Him as you pray. And let your prayers take as long as they need to take. Focus on communication rather than agendas, schedules, or limits.

❧

The birds that fly highest
are the birds of "pray."

Grow Closer to God,

I Would . . .

Realize that intimacy with Him takes time.

And Jesus grew in wisdom and stature, and in favor with God and men.
—Luke 2:52

We live in an age of immediate gratification, with its instant coffee, Minute Rice, and microwave dinners. Even first-class mail is now called "snail mail." We must realize that there is no instant formula for intimacy with God. Some have sought it, only to give up in discouragement.

Relationships take time. And the very idea of growing closer to God evokes a process: learning more about Him, growing more aware of His presence in your life, and becoming more confident in His love and power. So take the time to get to know God. And leave the instant gratification to the coffee people.

&

Growing in personal relationship with
God is a marathon, not a forty-yard dash.

Grow Closer to God,

I Would . . .

Strive to be a saint, not a celebrity.

For whoever exalts himself will be humbled, and whoever humbles himself will be exalted.
—Matthew 23:12

To some, life is a theater in which they play the role of celebrity. They flaunt their talents and accomplishments, even their super-spirituality. They are like the Pharisees of Jesus' day, who made a big production even out of fasting. They wanted everyone to be impressed by their long, hungry faces.

All people do this in one way or another, lurking behind masks that cloak their insecurities or hide selfish agendas. The walk of faith is no place for masks. It's a place for naked faces, blemishes and all. A place where people look each other in the eye, and look to God for guidance, hope, and forgiveness.

The world has enough celebrities. It could use a few more saints.

Grow Closer to God,

I Would . . .

Remember that Heaven is a real place.

*The world has forgotten,
in its concern with Left and Right,
that there is an Above and Below.*
—Glen Drake

A young man completing a job application came to the line asking for his "permanent address." He thought for a moment, then wrote "Heaven." He understood that heaven is a real place—and ultimately, it will be his home and the home of all those who put their trust in God.

You will be more conscious of God in your everyday life if you remember—like the young man—that He is the landlord of your permanent home. Someday you will actually meet Him. How you will feel about that experience depends on how you spend your time here in your temporary home—earth.

❧

What's ahead of us is far better
than anything that's behind us.

Grow Closer to God,

I Would . . .

Stop sweating the small stuff.

❧

*Who of you by worrying can
add a single hour to his life?*
—Matthew 6:27

It's amazing how minor irritations can take our eyes off God. Tension headaches interrupt our sleep. Telemarketers interrupt our dinner. Car troubles interrupt our vacations. At times like these, we must step back and regain perspective. What is a traffic ticket or flat tire or cold sore compared with being loved purely and eternally by almighty God?

Take your worries to God in prayer and *leave* them there. If you find that difficult to do, remember that you are entrusting your cares to the One who hung the stars and set the planets in motion, the One who created the earth and all that is in it. He should be able to handle whatever you bring before Him.

Worry is the interest paid by
those who borrow trouble.

Grow Closer to God,

I Would . . .

Stop holding out on Him.

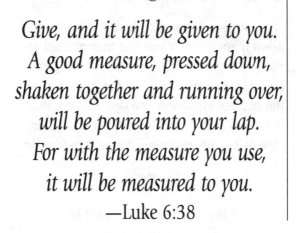

Give, and it will be given to you.
A good measure, pressed down,
shaken together and running over,
will be poured into your lap.
For with the measure you use,
it will be measured to you.
—Luke 6:38

To be near God, you don't have to be perfect. But there is one requirement: you must totally submit yourself to Him. That means nothing held back—unconditional surrender. Just as you can't be "mostly married" or "somewhat pregnant," you cannot think of God as a "nodding acquaintance." Relationship with God simply doesn't work that way.

If you choose to hang onto some area of your life, will God still love you? Of course! He loved you long before you were even aware of Him. But, if you truly want to grow close to God, to know Him as a friend, you must give yourself completely into His care.

To be holy, you must be wholly His.

Grow Closer to God,

I Would . . .

Open my

heart.

*Paradise is open to
all receptive hearts.*
—Olivia Kent

Life's pain and disappointment can cause us to close our hearts tight like a fist. Or we may close our hearts to hold on to something we fear losing. Unfortunately, a tense heart can't relax, can't laugh, can't truly love. And it can't fully receive God's love.

An open heart signals a readiness for whatever changes, surprises, and gifts God has to offer. Picture your heart as a door—a door that you can leave open for God. After all, He is the One who built the door and the house. And He has already made it clear that He wants to come in and stay with you forever.

❧

A heart open to God is a heart open to good.

Travel light.

❧

Whoever loves money never
has money enough; whoever
loves wealth is never
satisfied with his income.
—Ecclesiastes 5:10

Many Americans have a possession obsession—laptop computers, digital TVs, cell phones, sports cars. These items aren't inherently bad, but they can easily become sources of security, even of pride.

Jesus taught His followers to travel light. To take with them only what they would need for their journey. He reminded them to concentrate on the grace of His Spirit—and not to be distracted by the glitter of shiny things. Why? Because the light of God's divine love is so brilliant that it makes everything else pale in comparison. If you want to really know Him, don't get distracted by worldly possessions.

❧

*The excess baggage of materialism always
makes the journey more difficult.*

Grow Closer to God,

I Would . . .

Remember that it pays to praise.

Doth not all nature around me praise God? If I were silent, I should be an exception to the universe.

—Charles H. Spurgeon

One of the Bible's most reassuring promises is found in Psalm 22:3, which says that God inhabits the praise of His people. This is a rather mysterious concept, but we can be confident that when we praise God, when we commend Him, when we express our esteem for Him, somehow His presence is there.

So come closer to God. Adore Him. Thank Him. Praise Him. Celebrate Him. Worship Him in whatever way best expresses what's in your heart. Talk to Him. Sing to Him. Or lift your eyes toward heaven and simply smile at Him. And He will be there with you.

Our praise is one of God's favorite places to be.

Grow Closer to God,

I Would . . .

Keep a spiritual journal.

*The only important thing
a writer needs is a subject.*
—Brooks Atkinson

Your relationship with God is worth writing home about. Record your thoughts, discoveries, applications, questions, goals. Putting these things in writing helps make them more tangible—and probably easier to remember. Another benefit of the spiritual journal is that you can look back on it and note the progress you've made in your relationship with God. You can see how He's made clear what once was confusing. And you can recall how He has answered your prayers.

When you want someone to stand behind a promise or statement he has made, you may say, "Put it in writing." If you value your relationship with God, do likewise.

A spiritual journal is a great way to chronicle your spiritual journey.

Grow Closer to God,

I Would . . .

Admire His creation.

*The heavens declare the
glory of God; the skies proclaim
the work of his hands.*
—Psalm 19:1

Just as the vision, passion, and talent of a great painter can be seen in his art, God has revealed Himself to us through His creation. We should allow ourselves to be awed and moved by the intricacy, wonder, and beauty of God's handiwork. The expanse of the sky filled with stars. The vastness of the oceans. The marvel of the human body.

And remember, the all-powerful Master Creator of the universe loves you and wants to have a personal relationship with you. He desires it so much that He has painted a magnificent masterpiece in His creation to draw you to His side.

*The universe is God's work of art,
and work of heart.*

Say "Phooey"

to fear.

*Do the thing that you fear,
and the death of fear is certain.*
—American Proverb

God is an authority figure, and some of us fear authority figures. We may picture an angry father or a harsh teacher or coach. Perhaps one of these people abused his or her power, we've never forgotten it, and now we're afraid to get too close to God. We remember the wounds of the past. We're not sure we can ever trust again.

If that is where you find yourself, fear not! God will not betray you, disappoint you, or abuse you. Remember what He did for you. He has proven His love and trustworthiness. No one who has trusted God and become close to Him has ever been disappointed.

If you find your knees knocking, kneel on them.

Grow Closer to God,

I Would . . .

Heed His correction.

*Whoever heeds
correction is honored.*
—Proverbs 13:18

The Bible notes that God reproves those He loves. He isn't out to ruin us or make us pay. He simply wants to protect us from the disasters our willfulness often creates. How does He correct us? We may hear His voice speaking deep within, through our consciences. Or God may urge someone to speak a word of truth to us. He also attempts to steer us back on course by allowing us to suffer the consequences of our actions.

However they come to you, God's reproofs are like mirrors, reminding you when your face is dirty and needs cleaning. Take a look. And if you see something that needs fixing, with God's help—fix it.

God's correction is always correct.

Grow Closer to God,

I Would . . .

Memorize a
verse a week.

*I used to have trouble
memorizing stuff, before I read
that book by what's his name.*
—Drew Cody
(in *The Stand-Up Guy*)

You probably won't have a Bible at your fingertips every moment of your life. But you can have God's wisdom "at the ready" if you commit to memorizing just one verse a week. You may think you're not good at memorizing, but you can probably recite a few key verses already—not to mention the "Pledge of Allegiance" and most of the words to "The Star-Spangled Banner."

As you memorize each verse, think about its implications, how you might apply it in everyday life. Armed with God's Word in your mind and heart, you'll feel much closer to God and better prepared to make wise choices.

❦

Ask God to help you recall Scriptures, and don't forget to say, "Thanks for the memories."

Grow Closer to God,

I Would . . .

Read Christian magazines.

❧

*Finally, brothers, whatever is
true, whatever is noble, whatever
is right, whatever is pure,
whatever is lovely, whatever is
admirable—if anything is
excellent or praiseworthy—
think about such things.*
—Philippians 4:8

If you've passed by a newsstand recently, you've probably noticed the variety of magazines available. Whether you're a scuba diver, chocolate lover, or dirt-bike rider, there's a magazine for you.

But what you may not know is that there are dozens of Christian magazines tailored to a variety of interests. You can read about Christian music, Christian athletes, or Christian media personalities. There are even magazines for worship leaders and biblical archaeology buffs. Take the time to investigate what's available. You'll probably find a publication that addresses your passion for your hobby or area of interest—and your passion for God.

It's worth checking out the magazine scene.

Grow Closer to God,

I Would . . .

Avoid
screening
God's calls.

He calls his own sheep by name.
—John 10:3

We spend much of our lives in front of screens. Computer screens, TV screens, movie screens. Some of this screen time is unavoidable, but think about how much time you can waste in front of various screens. A little channel surfing or Web surfing can subtly turn into hours that leave you with little more than glazed eyes and sore buns.

What's worse, screen time can gobble up hours that could be put to better use—time with God, family, or friends. Time is one of the most valuable possessions you will ever have. Don't waste it. Invest it in things of lasting value by committing to carefully screening your screen time.

Screening out God can leave you spiritually empty.

Grow Closer to God,

I Would . . .

Remember that God did the choosing.

৽৶

For he [God] chose us in him before the creation of the world to be holy and blameless in his sight.
—Ephesians 1:4

Remember the thrill of being picked first for a sports team? Or the agony of being picked last—or ending up on a team purely by default? One of the beautiful things about a life in close relationship with God is knowing that we have been chosen first for His team.

God chose you long before you chose Him—before you decided that you wanted to be close to Him. In fact, the Bible says that He chose you even before the foundations of the earth were set in place. That's right! God chose you first, and even the little prodding in your heart that made you want to know Him, came from Him. Even your faith is His gift.

If God didn't choose, we'd lose.

Grow Closer to God,

I Would . . .

Treat my body like a temple, not a bowling alley.

Activity strengthens.
Inactivity weakens.
—Hippocrates

If an esteemed guest came to live with you, what accommodations would you provide? Wouldn't you try to make your home as inviting and pleasant as possible? The Bible teaches that our bodies are the temples of God's Spirit. That means that as we grow close to God, eventually we invite Him to come and live within us—just as when a couple makes their vows of marriage and thereafter live together in the same house.

Is your temple an appropriate dwelling place for God? You don't have to be a model or an Olympic athlete, but your body is a gift from God. So honor Him by treating it right.

❧

Guarding your health shows
respect for your Creator.

Grow Closer to God,

I Would . . .

Obey the Ten Commandments.

❦

You shall have no other gods before me.
You shall not make for yourself an idol. . . .
You shall not bow down to them or worship them. . . .
You shall not misuse the name of the LORD your God. . . .
Remember the Sabbath day by keeping it holy. . . .
Honor your father and your mother. . . .
You shall not murder. You shall not commit adultery.
You shall not steal. You shall not give false
testimony against your neighbor.
You shall not covet.

—Exodus 20:3-17

Long before David Letterman, God created the original "Top Ten" list—His Ten Commandments. These rules for right living aren't allowed to be posted in some schools anymore, but they should be inscribed in our hearts and minds. The Ten Commandments are more than wise guidelines for living a holy and pleasing life; they also tell us much about God's character.

As you follow the Ten Commandments, you walk in step with their author, and His values become your values as well. Soon you will find yourself thinking like He thinks and doing what He would do. You will never know God completely—in many ways He is unknowable. But you can learn to walk by His side.

God's commandments are a perfect ten.

Grow Closer to God,

I Would . . .

Keep my promises to Him.

*We must not promise what we
ought not, lest we be called to
perform what we cannot.*
—Abraham Lincoln

Have you ever promised God you would do something—or stop doing something—then later forgotten about the promise or brushed it aside? Promises to a holy God shouldn't be taken lightly. Unkept promises create walls between us and our Creator, because we lose our confidence and draw back from His love and blessing.

So don't make vows to God without thinking them through very carefully. When you promise Him something, keep your promise. When you have learned to honor God in this way, you will find it much easier to keep your promises to the earth dwellers in your life.

Your relationship with God should be built on promises, not compromises.

Truly worship Him.

*The life of man consists
in beholding God.*
—St. Irenaeus

True worship isn't about religious rituals, but rather the pure and genuine expression of praise from a willing and eager heart. Children have much to teach us in this regard. They come to us without agendas, without pretension, without motives. They come with true hearts. It is close to impossible to walk away untouched by these unfettered affirmations, and God finds our true worship equally as compelling.

Choose any method you like to worship God. singing, reading Scripture, praying aloud, or by simple and silent reverence—there are a limitless number of ways. No matter how you choose to go about it, remember to do so with the heart of a child.

❧

Worship is to the Christian life what the mainspring is to a watch.

Remember that God loves all His children.

*In humility consider others
better than yourselves.*
—Philippians 2:3

It might be easy to believe that God loves you or Billy Graham or some other great leader, but what about that frightful-looking rock star or dishonest politician? Do you tend to believe that God must love you more than them?

God loves all His children, though He grieves over those who choose not to respond to His love and care. So the next time you see someone offensive to you, remember: God loves that person no less than He loves you, or Billy Graham, or one of the saints of old. If you want to be close to God, you must learn to love the unlovely.

❧

God's hand is extended to all mankind.

Remember that money and material goods are immaterial.

*Money has never yet
made anyone rich.*
—Seneca

It's ironic that money carries the words "In God We Trust," because wealth—or the pursuit of it—can hinder our trust in God. Money and possessions can never truly satisfy the human soul. A guy named Solomon tried that route and was left empty.

Only God can establish your self-worth and fulfill your deepest longings. Only relationship with Him can make you alive to His love, aware of your life's purpose, and filled with inner peace. And unlike money, God will never disappear, be taken away, or lose His value. Remember that money may rule the world's economy but it takes a back seat in God's economy.

*Remember, it's "In God We Trust,"
not "In Gold We Trust."*

Use my talents.

*Abilities are like tax
deductions—we either use
them or we lose them.*
—Sam Jennings

God has given each of us abilities. If we develop these skills, we can then use them in a way that will benefit others and bring glory to our Creator. What about your skills? Are you using them? Or are they lying dormant, gathering dust?

Putting your God-given talents to work is one of the most satisfying things you can do. As you do what God created you to do, you gain a deep sense of purpose—and you become closer and more grateful to the One who gave you your talents. There are few things as beautiful as Creator and creation working hand in hand.

Do what you can with what you've been given.

Be willing to search for Him.

We saw his star in the east and have come to worship him.
—Matthew 2:2

The wise men's friends must have questioned if they were really wise. Here were these fellows, following only hearsay and one bright star on a long journey—a journey filled with unanswered questions and many risks. But their long search was rewarded when they found the child king, offered their gifts, and expressed their deep and humble adoration.

Even today, the wise men can be our guides, our examples. Their story can be your story. Are you willing to take the journey—whether physical, intellectual, or spiritual—that will lead you into God's presence?

We may no longer ride camels, but wise men and women still seek God.

Grow Closer to God,

I Would . . .

Listen to Christian music.

❧

*The LORD is my strength
and my song.*
—Psalm 118:14

Today's Christian music offers something for every taste—from classical to hip-hop to heavy metal. But regardless of their musical style, Christian artists have a common purpose: to glorify God through their music, to celebrate life, and to share some of their most honest moments before God. Some artists have revealed that when they are recording, they feel a deep and real sense of God's anointing.

You can share in that anointing as you share in their music. Visit a bookstore and choose something in harmony with your own personal taste. And then, take some time to listen up and let your soul soar!

Christian music can bring us
into harmony with God.

Celebrate my individuality.

*I thank God for my handicaps,
for, through them, I have found
myself, my work, and my God.*
—Helen Keller

God didn't make you like anyone else on the entire planet. Even identical twins aren't truly identical. God made you unique, and He has unique plans for you and your talents— and even your limitations.

That's why you must never put yourself down because you are not like everyone else. Instead revel in your individuality and thank your Creator who had the inspiration and foresight to make you exactly the way you are. You are special because He has made you so, and understanding that will draw you closer to Him.

God's children are fearfully and wonderfully formed in their mothers' wombs, not mass-produced on an assembly line.

Grow Closer to God,

I Would . . .

Think small.

*Who despises the day
of small things?*
—Zechariah 4:10

Our world loves bigness. Large, economy-sized boxes of detergent. Super-sized meals. Vehicles with extra leg room and extra head room. God is certainly capable of big feats. He parted the Red Sea. He created the universe in less than a week. But He also used only a small army to defeat the Midianites and fed a whole multitude of people from one boy's small lunch. And He sent a tiny baby to save the world.

Don't measure your success by how well-known you are or how much money you have. God isn't impressed with your bigness. He is interested in your life and the small but faithful steps you take toward Him each day.

Little things make a big difference to God.

Remember that I don't look good in green.

Envy takes the joy, happiness, and contentment out of living.
—Billy Graham

God hates jealousy so much that He
mentioned it in two of His Ten Commandments.
We are all God's creation. He loves us all,
and we shouldn't compare our "blessings"
with those of others. When we envy what
others have, we rob ourselves of the joy and
contentment we should find in what God has
given us.

Guard your heart. If you find that you are
unable to rejoice over the success of others,
beware. Instead of focusing on what others
have, ask God to remind you of the many
blessings He has given you--and how many
of them are undeserved.

❧

God's children should be zealous, not jealous.

Learn to take "no" for an answer.

*God always answers prayer, but
His answer isn't always, "yes."*
—Olivia Kent

God is not Santa Claus. Nor is He a heavenly vending machine that dispenses goodies on demand. God doesn't give us all we ask for. Remember, Jesus' prayer to have the cup of death taken from Him? Even Christ Himself didn't get affirmative answers to all of His prayers.

Remember that God does *hear* every prayer, but He may decide it is best not to answer in the way you hope He will. Be open-hearted at these times. You may learn more about God and His will for your life from the "no" and "wait" answers than you do from the times He provides exactly what you ask for.

❧

God's answer isn't always yes,
but it is always perfect.

Grow Closer to God,

I Would . . .

Avoid relying on emotions.

❧

Now faith is being sure of what we hope for and certain of what we do not see.

—Hebrews 11:1

Emotions are wonderful. They add flavor and heat to life. They make us feel more alive. Emotions, however, make lousy foundations for our faith in God because they can be radically affected by things like diet, lack of sleep, and internal chemistry. You shouldn't look to your feelings to judge whether God loves You. Your assurance isn't from getting goose bumps or chills down your spine—after all, the flu can provide that.

Thank God that His love for us isn't based on how we *feel;* it's based on His integrity. His promises remain true regardless of how we feel about them.

❦

God's love is more than a feeling; it's a fact.

Grow Closer to God,

I Would . . .

Remember that I'm part of His relay team.

We have received the baton of faith. We must pass it carefully on to the next generation.
—Taylor Morgan

One responsibility of a close relationship with God is to pass on to others the wisdom and inspiration you receive from your walk with Him. Just as you will almost certainly benefit from the encouragement of those who have walked with God before you, now you must run your relay leg with vigor and care—then pass on the memory of God in your life to others.

If you don't do your part, that memory will fade, and future generations will be deprived of a sense of history and knowledge of God's faithfulness to those who seek Him and find Him throughout the ages.

Don't forget to keep the memory of God alive.

Grow Closer to God,

I Would . . .

Stop worrying and be hopeful.

*Worry is the misuse
of the imagination.*
—Anonymous

In Philippians 4, Paul instructs us to "be anxious for *nothing.*" Think about that. Paul says the child of God shouldn't worry about anything! And Paul didn't give this advice lightly. He was in prison at the time he wrote it. But despite all his trials, Paul knew God could bring peace. God doesn't always untie all the knots in our lives. But He does give us the grace to live with the knots.

So remember, there is nothing you face that is too difficult, too troubling, or too frightening for God. He holds the world in the palm of His hand. Your problems aren't likely to stump Him.

Turn your worries over to God, and let His perfect peace guide your heart.

Grow Closer to God,

I Would . . .

Go to Him
in times
of trouble.

God is our refuge and strength,
a very present help in trouble.
—Psalm 46:1 KJV

Some of the closest relationships are forged in times of crisis—on the battlefield, in the hospital, or during a natural disaster. Yet many people run from God—out of anger or despair—when calamity occurs, forfeiting a wonderful opportunity to grow closer to Him.

If you're tempted to flee from God in times of trouble, know that He never loses control of any situation. He knows what He is doing or allowing to happen. So once You have found Him, don't leave His protection. Cling to your fellowship with Him. Remember, every good father wants his children to rely on him when pain and disaster strike.

When you face trouble,
go to God on the double.

Let go of
past failures.

*The greatest failure
is the failure to try.*
—William Ward

As imperfect people, we make mistakes. We drop the ball, miss the mark, fall on our faces, use too many clichés. Failure can make us feel inadequate, especially when we compare ourselves to others who seem to be living more effectively.

When you feel like a failure compared to others, remember your proper motivation for life: You have chosen to live in close fellowship with God out of your love for Him rather than to impress an audience of your peers. Focus on God, and know that He will cheer you on—and pick you up and dust you off when you fall. And He won't hold your failures against you, so don't hold them against yourself.

❦

*Glory isn't in never failing, but
in rising every time you fall.*

Grow Closer to God,

I Would . . .

Welcome
trials.

In the presence of trouble,
some grow wings.
Others buy crutches.
—American Proverb

When athletes train hard, they run or lift weights to the point of muscle failure. This approach actually breaks down muscle fibers, which would seem to be a detriment to performance. However, it's beneficial because the body adapts to the stress and rebuilds the damaged fibers stronger than ever before.

This principle is also important to our spiritual strength and stamina. God does not cause our pain and struggle, but He does allow a certain amount of adversity to come into our lives. His purpose is to see that we grow strong and resilient rather than weak and complacent. So smile when you encounter trials. See them as opportunities to grow strong in your faith and closer to God.

Don't be guilty of giving trials an unjust verdict.

Put away
my gavel.

*Do not judge,
or you too will be judged.*
—Matthew 7:1

Judges today are celebrities. Some even have their own television shows where they scold, cajole, and sentence those who come before them. Sometimes it's tempting to put on the long black robes ourselves and pass judgment on others. It's easy for us to see their faults and pronounce them "Guilty!" There's only one problem. Being judgmental is courting disaster.

When you pronounce verdicts on others, you open yourself up to the same kind of prosecution. So leave the judging to God. And when you see others misbehaving, thank God for His mercy, which is available to all and free for the asking.

Sitting high in the judgment seat keeps you from getting on your knees.

Grow Closer to God,

I Would . . .

Look in the mirror and say, "Hello, masterpiece."

So God created man in his own image, in the image of God he created him, male and female he created them.
—Genesis 1:27

Ephesians 2:10 tells us that we are "God's workmanship, created in Christ Jesus to do good works." That means we are God's works of art. Imagine that. You are the creation of the only perfect artist in the universe. And the news just keeps getting better. God didn't craft you merely to sit around collecting dust in some cosmic art gallery. He created you for a purpose—His purpose.

So next time your self-esteem takes a hit, and you think you aren't important enough, smart enough, sophisticated enough, charming enough, rich enough, or good-looking enough to draw close to God, remember who you are—God's work of art. God's *functional* work of art.

⚛

*God's works of art are built
for action, not auction.*

Quit trying to shrink Him.

Your God is too small!
—J. B. Phillips

Many people like to reduce God to something small and simple enough for their finite minds to understand. But God's ways are not our ways. And we can get so caught up in a destination called "Complete Understanding" that we forget to enjoy the journey.

Think of how many times Jesus answered a question with another question—or didn't deliver when people demanded, "Show us a sign!" Maybe He was trying to teach us something—that the *search* for God matters more than arriving at the mistaken notion that we've brought Him down to our level and captured His essence. Maybe it's the search itself that makes us who we are.

❧

God doesn't fit well in small boxes of human invention.

Fly with eagles rather than crawl with slugs.

He who walks with the wise grows wise, but a companion of fools suffers harm.
—Proverbs 13:20

Companionship choices are difficult. Jesus spent time with many people of low reputation. Yet the Bible cautions us that bad company corrupts good character. The key to following Jesus' example *and* protecting ourselves lies in discernment. Follow these simple guidelines.

First, spend as much time as possible with godly people who will encourage you to grow closer to God. Second, as you befriend troubled people, be careful to do so on your terms, as much as possible. And third, you must constantly ask yourself, "Am I drawing these people toward God, or are they drawing me away?"

༄

Keep in mind that it's easier to be pulled down than to be pulled up.

Begin to appreciate His passions.

*The LORD is gracious and
compassionate, slow to
anger and rich in love.*
—Psalm 145:8

God is not an emotionless robotic power. The Bible says that God has intense feelings—sorrow over those who choose to live without His love and joy over those who turn from their destructive paths. If you want to grow closer to God, ask Him to let you feel a part of what He feels.

Imagine what a privilege it would be to glimpse inside the holy and eternal heart of God. To feel His godly compassion for suffering humanity. To feel His righteous indignation for those who are treated unjustly. To feel His fatherly delight when one of His children hurries to spend time with Him. It would surely change your life.

We strive to empathize with family and friends, why not also with God?

Grow Closer to God,

I Would . . .

Go to church.

*Let us not give up
meeting together.*
—Hebrews 10:25

If you are serious about growing closer in your relationship with God, then it is vitally important that you find a church home where you feel comfortable and attend regularly. Meeting together with other believers provides encouragement and instruction as you walk the road of faith.

Once you find the right congregation, take time to get to know those you see every week. Take time to learn about the services and programs your church can provide. Get involved with the activities your church provides for church members and the community as a whole. You will be blessed by the support and comfort a church family can provide.

Sorrows are diminished and joys multiplied when you share them.

Grow Closer to God,

I Would . . .

Respond
immediately
to His calling.

What I mean, brothers,
is that the time is short.
—1 Corinthians 7:29

The Bible tells us to "redeem the time" (Ephesians 5:16 KJV). That means that we should make the most of every opportunity, because some don't linger for long. So when we feel a prompting from our heavenly Father, we should never say, "Leave a message, and I'll get back to You later." Remember, God has legions of angels who will do whatever He asks. He wants us to share in His divine activity for *our* benefit, not His.

It's our loss when we miss the opportunity to serve Him. So respond immediately when you hear God speak. His will is perfect, and His plans for you always lead to abundant life.

❧

The time you kill can never be resuscitated.

Grow Closer to God,

I Would . . .

Realize there is nowhere He won't go.

If the Lord be with us, we have no cause of fear. His eye is upon us, His arm over us, His ear open to our prayer—His grace sufficient, His promise unchangeable.
—John Newton

"Don't go there" is one of the most overused phrases of the late 1990s. But it doesn't apply to God. He never sends His children anywhere alone. In Old Testament times, He was with them as a pillar of fire, a cloud, a burning bush, or a voice from heaven. Today, He is with us in the form of His Holy Spirit, the Bible, and godly leaders and friends.

So, if you're enduring trials, remember that the Lord has gone before you and is also with you now. He knows what you are facing—He has even endured death—and He's ready to respond to your need.

❧

Rest in the knowledge that you cannot go where God cannot reach.

Meditate on His Word.

A man of meditation is happy,
not for an hour or a day,
but quite round the
circle of all his years.
—Isaac Taylor

Some people are frightened by the word *meditation.* It evokes images of bearded gurus sitting cross-legged in robes and chanting meaningless monosyllables. However, to meditate simply means to think deeply and continuously about something.

For the person who wants to grow closer to God, meditation can consist merely of focusing on the Bible's teachings and the God behind them. It's letting Him fill your mind and heart—and even the farthest corner of your soul. Meditate on God's goodness, on His wisdom and counsel, on His love and kindness. Meditate on His awesome creation and wondrous works. It doesn't matter what aspect of God you choose, meditating on Him will transform your life.

Don't hesitate to meditate.

Dedicate my efforts to Him.

*Commit thy works unto
the LORD, and thy thoughts
shall be established.*
—Proverbs 16:3 KJV

Legendary college football coach Knute Rockne gleaned a marvelous performance from his team one time by urging them to "win one for the Gipper," a deceased former player. How much more motivation can we muster by dedicating our efforts to the God who created us and loves us eternally.

Whether you're doing something athletic, artistic, or career-oriented, do it for God. Dedicate everything you do to God as a gesture of appreciation for the talents He has placed in your life. Then, however your efforts turn out, you will know the joy of pleasing and honoring Him.

⁂

Give it all you've got for God.

Grow Closer to God,

I Would . . .

Remember.

*When memory makes
a journey into the past we live
not once, but twice, the
best times of our lives.*
—E. C. Rayburn

"You're only as good as your last game" is a popular adage in sports today. And a hit song a few years ago asked the question, "What have you done for me lately?" Look at the story of the Israelites in the Old Testament. They forgot about how God had parted the Red Sea and delivered them from their oppressors. A short while after that miraculous event, they were worshipping a golden statue of a calf.

It's important to remember all God has done for you—all the love, mercy, and answered prayers that have brought you to this point in your life. That same God will be with you in the future, and that means all of eternity.

❧

Too many people have short memories and long lists of wants.

Grow Closer to God,

I Would . . .

Concentrate on being faithful, not successful.

*Let love and faithfulness
never leave you.*
—Proverbs 3:3

In contemporary society, people are judged by numbers—how much money they grossed last year, how many new clients they brought in. Given the world's view of success, it's easy to assume God thinks the same way. Thus, people sometimes focus on church attendance, number of volunteer activities, or the amount of money they put in the offering as the ways to please Him.

God is not some great statistician in the sky. He's more concerned with the state of your heart than how many good deeds you perform. So focus on simply being faithful to Him, and success will take care of itself.

If at first you don't succeed,
be faithful and keep trying.

Grow Closer to God,

I Would . . .

Be unafraid
of age.

*It's not how old you are,
but how you are old.*
—Marie Dressler

Vitamins. Nutritional supplements. Mud packs. Face creams. Face lifts. Miracle diets. America abounds with weapons to fight old age. And with good reason—some people fear aging more than they fear monsters or even an IRS audit.

Yet age is not an enemy to you, the child of God. You are eternal. So view your time as a chance to grow closer to Him, to store up treasures in heaven, and to bring a bit of heaven to life on earth. And never forget that your ultimate destiny is with your Father—with an ageless body in a timeless paradise.

There are none so old as those who have outlived their enthusiasm and lost their perspective.

Grow Closer to God,

I Would . . .

Never wrongly accuse Him.

*How great is your goodness,
which you have stored up for
those who fear you, which you
bestow in the sight of men on
those who take refuge in you.*
—Psalm 31:19

Because God is all-powerful, it's possible to assume He causes *everything* that happens. But that isn't the case. People are responsible for their own actions. And there are other forces at work, wreaking pain and deceit on the world. That is not God's way. There are things He won't do. He won't tempt you to break the rules of right living, and He won't kick you when you're down.

If you're at odds with God over a perceived misdeed, realize that He doesn't do anything to make His children bitter. So let go of the resentment you harbor and ask forgiveness for your lack of faith. Be at peace with your perfect Father.

Fingers pointed in accusation at God would be better off folded in prayer.

Grow Closer to God,

I Would . . .

Listen to Him.

My sheep listen to my voice;
I know them, and
they follow me.
—John 10:27

It's impossible to have a close relationship without communication. And listening is vital. We must listen to God. He may not speak with a thundering voice from the heavens anymore, but neither is He silent. His voice is no less clear than it ever was. You may hear it through a Scripture passage, a sermon, a song on the radio, even the words of a child.

However God's voice comes to you, God's Spirit in you and your knowledge of the Scriptures will help you know when God is speaking to you. And remember to go beyond hearing His words—respond to them as well.

God hasn't lost His voice, but some people have lost the ability to listen.

Grow Closer to God,

I Would . . .

Turn away from prejudice.

•℣

*We must learn to live together
like brothers or we will
perish together like fools.*
—Martin Luther King Jr.

Jesus fervently prayed to God that believers "be brought to complete unity to let the world know that you sent me . . ." (John 17:23). Unfortunately, there are many things that hinder unity. Racism, for example, breeds hatred and misunderstanding and undermines the spiritual lives of believers.

Imagine what God thinks when some of His creation think they are better than others simply because of their skin color. Pray every day for racial harmony, and pursue relationships with people of different races. As you do this, you will help bring an answer to Jesus' prayer, and you can be sure that the heart of the God who plays no favorites will be with you.

To God, there is only one race: the human race.

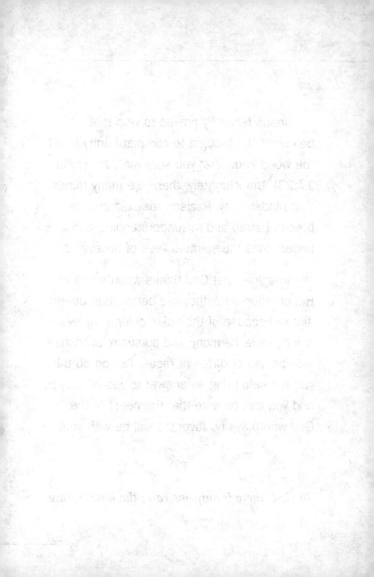

Additional copies of this book
and other books in this series are available
from your local bookstore.

If I Really Wanted to Be Happy, I Would . . .
If I Really Wanted to Lose Weight, I Would . . .
If I Really Wanted to Simplify My Life, I Would . . .

If you have enjoyed this book, or if it has
impacted your life, we would like to hear from you.
Please contact us at:

Honor Books
Department E
P.O. Box 55388
Tulsa, Oklahoma 74155
Or by e-mail at info@honorbooks.com

WILDERNESS FAMILY

PART 2

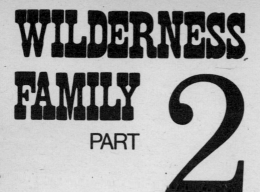

BY VIC CRUME
AND ARTHUR R. DUBS

SCHOLASTIC BOOK SERVICES
New York Toronto London Auckland Sydney Tokyo

Copyright © 1979 Wilderness Family, Inc. All rights reserved under International and Pan-American Copyright Conventions. Published by Scholastic Book Services, a division of Scholastic Magazines, Inc.

12 11 10 9 8 7 6 5 4 3   9/7 0 1 2 3 4/8

Printed in the U.S.A.   01

WILDERNESS FAMILY

FAMILY

PART

2

1

At the controls of the two-engine aquaplane, Stan Coble glanced at his passenger, Doctor Mike McCord. "Doc, you sure you know where you're going? I've never flown up this way before."

Mike McCord wasn't surprised by the pilot's question. As far as the eye could see, snow-capped mountain peaks jutted white against a brilliant blue sky. And in the wilderness valley below, autumn colors, red, orange, and gold, blazed all the brighter for the surrounding slopes of deep green pine forests.

Mike McCord chuckled. "And you're think-ing there's not a sight of human life anywhere — but I know this country like the back of my hand. Now just come right about five degrees. The lake will be over there — just a little beyond that ridge."

"*Another* mountain ridge!" Stan shook his head. "You say this Robinson fellow just bailed out of L.A. and moved his family way-the-heck to this wilderness? What's the matter with him? Does he hate people or something?"

"Doesn't hate anybody far as I know," Mike replied cheerfully. "Just hated smog and pollution and seeing his kids living in it. His little girl was really going downhill before they came here in the spring. And he was worn down from fighting traffic on the speedway. Told me he drove in it thirty miles a day just getting back and forth to his job."

Stan shrugged. "Well, I can understand how he felt. But Doc — summer up here is one thing. Winter? That's another." He looked down across the unbroken wilderness. "No roads. No stores —"

"No electricity. No indoor plumbing." Mike grinned. "And the nearest neighbor between here and Three Forks is twenty miles away *on foot*. Yep. That's about it. But Skip Robinson did what most guys just *dream* of doing. Got

2

himself a piece of land. Built himself a good cabin and ..." He broke off. "Here's the lake. Now just up ahead on the right you can see the little dock."

Near the sapphire blue lake they could see the Robinson cabin; a wisp of white smoke curling from the chimney. Stan nosed down in a long, curving swoop, and then the plane was skimming the mirror-like lake surface.

"Here comes the welcoming committee," Mike laughed. "See — over there on the hill meadow? That's Jenny. She's twelve. And right in there racing her — that's Toby. He's nine. Or is it ten?"

"Looks like the dog's going to beat them both."

"That's Crust," Mike said. "He's a real member of the family. They have a few other family members you'll probably meet — a pet raccoon and a black bear they call Samson. Samson was the former owner's and he settled right down with them." He laughed. "Just want you to have everybody's name straight. Mrs. Robinson's is 'Pat' and Skip is —"

"Skip, I bet." Stan cut the engines. "You sure seem to like this family, Doc."

"Great folks!" Mike beamed. "You'll see."

Stan could honestly say, "I've heard a lot

about you," when he met each member of the Robinson family. And he couldn't remember a more enthusiastic welcome in his whole life. Jenny, Toby, and Crust immediately rushed Mike straight to the cabin, leaving Skip to help unload supplies.

Luckily, as Crust wasn't around to supervise, the job went fast. Skip helped Stan carry the last heavy box up the path to the cabin porch.

Skip turned to the pilot. "That landing you made was really neat. You came down like a bird!"

"Thanks. Could use a little more room in that lake. I wouldn't try it on skis after it ices over."

"No? Why not?"

Stan was blunt. "At this altitude, it's too dangerous to land in powder snow."

"Oh?" A faint frown creased Skip's forehead. "So that means after the first ice we won't be seeing you 'til spring, huh?"

"'Fraid so."

They thumped the box down on the porch.

Promptly, two black bear cubs came tumbling out from beneath the flooring. "Two more family members," Skip grinned. "Lost their mother in a rock slide last spring. Now

the problem's got to be how to get them —
er — *untamed*."

"Hi, there," called a voice from the doorway.

"Pat, meet Stan Coble," Skip smiled.

Pat didn't look like Stan Coble's idea of a rugged, pioneer wife fighting the great wilderness country. Pretty as her twelve-year-old daughter and not the least weatherbeaten, she held out a hand to her guest. "Welcome, Stan. How was your trip?"

"Pretty wild," he smiled back. "Hard to find you folks on a map."

Mike McCord stepped up from inside the cabin. "Pat, I haven't had the chance to tell you — you look fantastic! Honestly, you seem ten years younger."

She laughed. "That kind of talk will get you hot, fresh bread and some of our raspberry jam. Come on in, Stan."

"I'll slice the bread," Jenny said.

"And I'll get the jam," Toby volunteered.

"I'll put on the coffee pot," Pat laughed. "Skip — you round up Bandido and put him outside, will you?" She turned to Stan. "Bandido's our raccoon. We love him, but he loves our jam even more."

Stan noticed that each Robinson was an important part of whatever the family was doing. It pleased him to hear of "*our* jam." And he knew it would be "*our* lake, *our* cabin, *our* bear cubs." He looked across at Mike, spreading another delicious warm bread slice with "our jam." No wonder Mike McCord liked this family tucked away in the wilderness! Pat interrupted his thinking.

"Mike," she said, "don't spoil your appetite. We're having a big supper."

Doctor McCord lavished more raspberry jam on the bread slice. "Doggone it, Pat! You know I'd love nothing better. But Stan says weather is moving in behind us, and he wants to get back before it closes in."

"Then couldn't you stay over and fly out tomorrow?" Skip asked.

Before Stan could explain that weather "closing in" might mean weather closing in right over the Robinsons' snug cabin, Dr. Mike spoke up. "We'd love it, Skip, but I have an appointment tomorrow with a lady who's expecting a visit from the stork."

Toby set down his glass of powdered milk. He looked sternly at Dr. Mike. "You know we're too old for that stork stuff."

Dr. McCord laughed. "OK." He pushed back his chair. "Look at all of you! I've never seen such a healthy-looking family. What am I doing here, anyway?"

Toby beamed. "I guess that means we're not gonna get a shot?"

"No such luck," Doctor Mike told him. "Come on, Toby. You first. Let's get it over with."

Toby sighed. "Boy, that was dumb. Why did I have to bring up shots?"

His sister agreed. She pushed back her long brown hair. "Yes, Toby. That was dumb."

Doctor McCord's eyes twinkled. "Well, we brought a cure for 'dumb,' too. Kids, look in that big box over there."

School books! *And* school books! "Enough to last all winter," Doctor Mike grinned. "But cheer up, kids. There're ice skates, too. Jenny, I brought sewing kits for you and your mother, in case you want to whip up parkas, or something. And, Skip — here's something important for the whole family." He tugged out a fat paperback book. *"The Wilderness Almanac."* He grinned. "Tells you how to survive a winter up here."

Pat looked up quickly. "Survive?"

Hastily, Skip thumbed the pages. "Sure, Pat. Here's something on making snowshoes. Sounds like fun."

Doctor McCord set the last and smallest box on the table. "And this— It's a kind of wilderness medicine chest. Now, on any bottle marked with a red 'x,' better give me a call on your radio. They're a little powerful. So, hands off unless I say 'OK.' OK?"

"We sure appreciate this, Mike," Skip said, as their airborne family doctor swiftly completed Toby's and Jenny's shots.

"Don't mention it." Doctor McCord smiled. "Jenny, here, is my prize patient. Not a wheeze left in that chest, Jenny. Your dad did the right thing when he made the big move."

The doctor straightened up and turned to Skip and Pat. "I hope you know what you're getting into, friends. Winter can be rough. Sure you won't change your minds? I'll probably be flying up here again."

The children's father laughed. "Mike, please don't worry about us. We have our supplies. We have a two-way radio. What more could a wilderness family need?"

"Wings," Stan said firmly, "to fly south like the rest of us birds."

Only Jenny noticed the quick shadow pass across her mother's pretty face. "We *love* it here, Stan," she said quickly. "We wouldn't leave for *anything*!"

Toby bobbed his head. "Not for *anything*," he repeated. "Everything's already happened to us that could happen. And Jenny says we've got the most beautiful backyard in the whole world!"

Doctor Mike closed his satchel. "There's your answer, Stan," he laughed. "Well, folks, take care of yourselves and keep in touch."

But walking down to the docked seaplane, Doctor Mike McCord couldn't forget what he and Stan had seen on the flight out to the Robinson place. A file of bighorn sheep was heading down from the rocky ridges to winter on the lower ground, and a big bull elk stared up at them as much as to say, "That bird's heading the wrong way for this time of year." Now the doctor shrugged those thoughts away. If ever a man would look out for his family, Skip Robinson was the man. Besides, this was the age of the emergency helicopter, wasn't it?

With a big hug for Pat and the children, Doctor Mike said good-bye. "See you folks!"

Stan taxied the aquaplane out from the little dock. The Robinsons waved until their visitors, airborne, went humming out of sight.

2

Next morning was sparkling bright. The weather front Stan had worried about had not developed — at least, not as far as Jenny and Toby could notice. Their lake was smooth as glass — just right for Jenny's canoe paddling practice.

"Shall we take Crust along, Jenny?" Toby asked. "I bet he'd like a nice canoe ride. Wouldn't you, Crust?"

Jenny hesitated. "Well — if you promise to make him sit still, I guess it'd be all right."

At the lake edge an otter paused in his game of slide-down-the-bank. He stood as tall as he could and stared with great interest at Jenny's strange zig-zagging progress through the water.

"Hey, why do you keep changing directions?" Toby complained. "You're not getting us anywhere."

"Would you *please* sit still?" Jenny frowned. "You're spoiling my steering."

"Not either! You just don't paddle right."

Jenny pushed the paddle deep. The canoe tilted and swung, and Crust suddenly had an excellent view of the otter on the bank. The otter had just as good a look at Crust. And either he didn't like what he saw, or he figured he was too much in plain view, just sitting there. In a twinkling, like a super sort of magician, he made himself disappear. This was too much for Crust. He stretched forward to keep an eye on the circling ripples where the otter had vanished.

"Hold Crust, Toby!" Jenny yelled. "He'll tip us over!"

Now the curious otter popped up on the far side of the canoe. As far as he could see, this might turn into a better game than slide-down-the-bank. He bobbed down and popped up again a bit closer, and Crust proved equally willing to join in the otter's new game. He made a half-turn lunge, willing to take Toby right along with him if he cared to keep hanging on.

Two excited yells, one excited bark, and over the three went — much to the delight of the otter. He continued to watch the show from a safe distance, as Jenny, shoulder-deep in the chilling water, snatched up Toby. Crust, belatedly feeling his responsibility as a trusted family member, paddled fussily around as Jenny waded toward shore.

"I thought you could *handle* a canoe!" Toby exclaimed, teeth chattering.

"And I thought you promised to hold Crust!" Jenny retorted. She set Toby down to wade in the shallow water. "I've got to go all the way back and get that canoe — and *everything*."

"What's 'everything'? What's 'all the way back'? My gosh, you could almost reach the paddle from here."

In spite of sopping wet clothes and the chilly September air, the task of hauling the canoe up on the bank and turning it over to dry in the morning sun was exercise enough to warm the two, although they felt uncomfortably damp and steamy. Crust solved his wetness problem by a good showery shake. Then, lightheartedly, he set off for the cabin with not a guilty thought in his head.

Jenny and Toby followed squishily, each sorting out who was most to blame for the accident. Halfway up the path Jenny sighed. "I was *dumb*. You were *dumb*. Crust was *dumb*."

Toby sighed even louder. "Yeah. And you know what that means. Mom will say, 'I'm so thankful it happened so near shore.' And Dad will probably say, 'Yes. Nothing like being near shore when you take Crust with you.' And all the time you know what they're *really* saying."

Jenny nodded. "Yes. 'Dumb.' Then pretty soon *we* say it for them. 'We were dumb.' And that's *awful*. Well, let's get it over with." She dropped down on the steps when they reached the cabin and stripped off her shoes and socks.

Six months before, if Jenny had fallen into the cold lake, she would have ended up with pneumonia, or at least a cold that required a stay in bed. Now, in dry clothes, briskly toweling her long hair, Jenny glowed with health. The sight of her strong tanned daughter made Pat feel once more that all the hard work and the daily fight to win out over the savage wilderness had been worth it — worth every callus, blister, and heart-stopping adventure of the past few months.

"Toby, why don't you go help Dad," she

suggested. "He's out in the smokehouse."

"What's he smoking?" Toby asked.

"Moose. Naturally. You might say he's lay-ing in a supply of mooseburgers for winter. Smoking the meat will keep it from spoiling. Jenny, why don't you unpack our sewing kits? I hope Doctor Mike picked out ones with good strong button thread."

Good strong button thread didn't sound too exciting to Jenny, but neither did moosemeat smoking. She quickly set about exploring Doc-tor Mike's gifts.

Toby reached the smokehouse in time to see his dad start out, axe in hand, for the family woodpile. Toby would have liked swinging the big axe himself, but that was like wishing for Christmas in July. So he said nothing and took on his usual task of stacking wood for the stove and fireplace as his father split logs.

"When are you going to teach me to hunt, Dad?" he asked as the woodpile grew higher.

"Soon," his father answered, taking another well-aimed swing at a log.

"When's soon? Gosh, I could help get us meat if 'soon' was soon enough."

"Right. But first you learn how to hit a standing target."

Toby thought. "You mean like a bean can?"

"Yep. We'll soon need to wear snowshoes when we hunt, so we could start on that project tonight."

To Toby's disappointment, the drawings of snowshoes in the *Wilderness Almanac* looked more like stretched out tennis racquets than some magical way of skimming snowdrifts. When the first pair was finished, he clopped awkwardly around the cabin trying them out.

"Toby, you're supposed to *glide*," Jenny said.

"I'd like to see you *glide* on this floor."

"I'll glide when it snows," his sister replied loftily. "I'm waiting to learn at a *sensible* time."

Their mother yawned. "Speaking of learning — that reminds me. School starts tomorrow."

"School!" both Jenny and Toby exclaimed.

Pat laughed. "Well, don't go into shock, please. September — school. Remember?"

"I remember," Jenny said gloomily. "Oh, well — I guess we can't expect an adventure every day."

"I hope not," Pat murmured.

"What did you say, Pat?" Skip asked, looking up from the *Wilderness Almanac*.

"I said — er, bedtime, kids!"

15

At the end of the first "school" day, Pat Robinson watched her two children go galloping down to the lake shore. She turned from the window. "Skip — everybody makes mistakes, don't they?"

Skip looked up sharply from the *Wilderness Almanac*. "You mean it's a mistake to stay here this winter?" he asked.

"Oh, no. I mean it was a mistake to think that just because school starts this month in L.A. that it should start here. This weather is just too *precious*. But I hate to drop something I've started. It's a bad example for the children."

Skip laughed. "It's a good example. Shows the kids they've got a mother with good sense. I'll tell you what — at dinnertime I'll say the PTA has an announcement to make. Then you do the explaining."

Pat giggled. "Thanks for all your help. I'm sure the student body will be delighted."

"Well, it doesn't mean they can't learn anything. Let's make September and October how-to months, and save the books for real winter. OK?"

"Great idea. What do you have in mind?"

Skip hesitated. "Well — one thing. Toby's been begging me to show him how to handle a rifle. And —"

"*Skip*! He's not quite ten!"

Skip shook his head. "He's big enough to learn respect for a gun, Pat, and a little target shooting isn't going to hurt him."

"What about Jenny? She's not going to be too thrilled about learning how to bake biscuits, for instance, if Toby's out doing exciting things with you."

"Toby's been a tag-a-long long enough. No reason both kids shouldn't learn, but Jenny's always been *first*. She paddles the canoe. Toby just sits."

"Not very quietly," Pat laughed. "But, OK. I see your point."

For the first time that Toby Robinson could remember, nobody said, "Never mind, Toby... when you're a little older —"

All of a sudden, and when he least expected it, he must have become just a little older. He gazed over at the shiny bean can nailed to a tree trunk a hundred feet away. He carefully sighted along the barrel of the light-gauge rifle.

"Ok, now, Toby," his dad said. "That's the way you take aim and that's the way you tuck the gun butt — hard against your shoulder. Now give it to me and I'll show you how to load the magazine."

17

"Magazine!" Toby gasped. "Did we bring one?"

"Right here." Skip slapped the rifle. "That's the name of the part that holds the cartridges."

It didn't take long for Toby to learn what each part was for. Barrel, sights, butt, magazine, cartridge, safety catch, trigger. How to put all this information together in the right order was more important. Finally, the moment for loading, aiming, firing arrived.

"OK," Skip said. "Now the magazine is loaded, the gun is on 'safe' until you're ready to shoot. You understand, Toby?"

Toby nodded excitedly.

"And *remember* — never put a bullet in the firing chamber until you're ready to shoot. OK?"

Toby nodded again, too excited to speak.

"OK. Now push a cartridge into the firing chamber."

Toby pulled back the slide mechanism, then pushed it forward.

"OK. Ready to fire...right?"

"No, sir. First I gotta take the safety off."

"Good, Toby, OK. Now go ahead. Take aim. *Squeeze* the trigger — slow."

Hardly had Toby's shot rung out than a

voice from deep in the woods bellowed, *"Hold your fire!"*

"Holy cow!" Skip gasped, turning pale. "Somebody's in the woods!"

A mule brayed loudly. Then the sound of chickens squawking wildly mixed in with the braying and with a strange bleating sound. "Now hold on there, you dang blame critter!" a voice boomed.

Toby's face lighted up. "Dad! It's Boomer!"

And Boomer it was — the Robinsons' trapper friend whom they had first met in the summer. "Dad scat it," the big heavy Boomer scolded as he stepped into the clearing. A small menagerie trailed behind — chickens swung in crates over the mule's back, and a little nanny goat trailed behind. "What in tarnation you shootin' at, young'un?" Boomer called, pulling at his floppy hat. "I felt the wind of hot lead fan my ol' ear."

"Gee, I sure am sorry, Boomer," Toby cried out. "I was aiming at that tin can over there on that tree. I guess I missed it by a mile."

Boomer looked back and began walking to the target. "Now maybe I didn't feel anything too close, Toby. Looks to me as how I couldn't have." He held up the bean can.

Putting down the rifle, Toby sped toward

the tree. "Dad!" he yelled. "I hit it! I hit it! Wait'll I tell Jenny and Mom!" He streaked off down the meadow hill toward the cabin.

"That was pretty good shootin'," Boomer grinned, his glance following Toby's rush to report the news. "First time, you say?"

Skip nodded. He hesitated. "Boomer, I'd be obliged if you didn't mention to Pat how you were there just a bit back in the woods." He sighed. "She tries not to show her worries, but — Well, if she finds out how you just *might* have been hit, she'll be *seeing* newspaper headlines. You know — *Father helps son shoot visitor. Both face long prison sentences.*"

Boomer haw-hawed. "Missed me by a mile! That boy's got a good eye and a steady hand. But you're right. I won't worry the Missus. How is she, and that purty little Jenny?"

"Fine." Skip grinned. "Right now, I'm afraid Jenny's just getting over being mad at me. She wanted to be first to learn handling a rifle."

"Sakes! Don't blame her. And I bet she'll be as good as her brother."

Far from being mad, Jenny was bouncing in delight. She couldn't wait to put on a jacket before hurrying out to greet Boomer. "Am I glad you came back!" she exclaimed, giving him a big hug.

"By golly! You're a sight for sore eyes, Jenny. This here mountain air is makin' you grow like a weed! You two young'uns is my favorite sidekicks." He rummaged in the mule's saddlebags. "Flora here's been carryin' something for you."

He pulled out a hand-carved wooden flute and handed it to Toby. "There y'ar. Give us a tune, Toby. I made it myself outa an old willow reed. And, lemme see. These are for you, Jenny." He lifted up a string of bright-colored beads and slipped it over Jenny's neck. "Traded a beaver hide to an Indian down at Three Forks for them."

"They're *beautiful*!" Jenny exclaimed.

"And the chickens and nanny goat's for your ma and pa. The nanny goat — her name's Marybelle — she'll give you folks a nice cup of milk 'stead of that powdered kind you been drinkin'. And I might just come back and get her myself when you folks pack outta here for the winter."

"Oh, we're not leaving, Boomer," Jenny said. "But if you want Marybelle back —"

"Not *leavin'*?" Boomer frowned. "Well now!"

At the dinner table, Boomer finished his last sip of coffee. "That was mighty fine cookin', Missus Robinson," he said.

"Thanks, Boomer. Jenny made the biscuits for us."

"She *didn't*! Wal, if they weren't the finest I ever et you can call me 'Flora.'"

He pushed back his cup. "I jest hope ya know what you're in for," he said seriously. "I mean winter."

"Sure, Boomer!" Jenny smiled. "In California it'd rain for three whole days sometimes, the streets would get flooded and everything."

Boomer looked over at Jenny's father. "I mean — *real* winter. A rip-roarin', howlin' winter where it can get so cold it can freeze the skin right off your bones."

He flung his arms high. "One storm could dump 'nuff snow to cover up this here cabin. And that there lake will be lucky if it don't freeze five feet deep."

Boomer looked around the table. "And there's wolves. Now normally, wolves ain't no danger to people. They're right shy o' folks. But when everything's frozen up and they're starvin' — well —"

Skip glanced quickly at Pat's worried face. "Now, Boomer — let's be reasonable."

22

"I'm bein' reasonable," their guest said firmly. "Why, ol' Scarface himself might show up."

Wide-eyed, Toby asked, "Who's old Scarface?"

"Orneriest and ugliest old black wolf in these parts." He leaned back. "Well, I've warned ye."

Pat nodded. "And we appreciate it, Boomer."

"We sure do." Skip stood up. "In fact, we appreciate it so much that we're going to get our 'guest house' fixed up for you right now. You can stow your gear there."

Boomer knew the "guest house" was Jake's old cabin. Jake was Skip's uncle and the Robinsons had lived there until their new place was finished. He smiled. "Well, if it won't put you out none, maybe Flora and me could wait a coupla days afore we start our trapping over the ridge."

"A couple of *days*!" Jenny cried. "That's no visit at all!"

"That's right, Boomer," Skip smiled. "Thanksgiving's coming and you wouldn't want to miss Pat's turkey, would you?"

Boomer grinned. "Now that's some time off," he said shyly, pleased to be invited to a family feast.

"Right now we better relocate Samson," Skip said. "He's been making himself right at home lately."

"I shore hate to ask a bear to make other sleeping arrangements," Boomer said.

"He'll have to," Skip laughed. "He'll understand. He knows you're a member of our family!"

Samson did understand — but wasn't too pleased to be turned out of his usual nighttime residence. But he contented himself with merely giving Boomer a dirty look before shambling off in search of more peaceable quarters.

3

"Good morning, Boomer," Jenny cried out, the minute she saw their visitor step out from the old cabin.

Boomer yawned. "What d'you mean 'good morning'? I didn't sleep a wink all night what with your Pa a-having to rescue me from those bear cubs. Not to mention that pesky raccoon takin' a notion to share my bed."

Jenny giggled. "Dad told us. My goodness, Boomer! Our bear cubs wouldn't hurt you."

"No? Wal, I say bears is bears, and that's that. Now how about fetchin' a pail from your ma? Marybelle needs milkin'. I'll show you how to do it so's Marybelle won't miss me when I go."

Milking Marybelle turned out to be a hit performance with Bandido, the bear cubs, and the whole Robinson family. She rewarded her interested fans by bleating loudly and sticking her foot in the milk bucket.

"Don't know's I blame her," Boomer growled. "But there goes a nice day's supply." He got to his feet. "Skip, how's about us getting to work on a chicken pen? Or do you figgur on keepin' them in yore drawin' room, too?"

Skip grinned. "No, but it sure is handy when it comes to gathering eggs. Pat found one in a chair this morning and she's saving it for your breakfast."

"Shucks! She *ain't*!" Boomer exclaimed, blushing at being treated like company.

"We want to make it up to you for last night," Jenny said. "But tonight's going to be just *lovely*. We promise."

It was a promise the Robinsons couldn't keep.

Moonlight streamed along the lake unnoticed by the snoozing Robinsons and their guest, when, in the deep shadows, a squat, dark animal moved cautiously toward the new chicken pen.

The meanest, most vicious, vilest-tempered creature of the forest was on the move.

Pound-for-pound the wolverine is the most terrible fighter of the wild. That ugly prowler had little to fear, and a lot to gain, from chickens.

Marybelle gave the first alarm, bleating in fright. Flora set up a loud braying. The chickens beat their wings and clucked nervously. In the cabin, Crust growled at the doorway.

"What's wrong, Skip?" Pat asked sleepily, half sitting up.

"Ssh. Something's after the chickens. I'm going out with Crust." He reached for his rifle.

Holding the dog by the collar, Skip tiptoed around the back of the cabin. "Hush, Crust!"

But in a flash, the wolverine, not intending to be cheated out of his meal, was over the fence and into the pen. Crust jerked loose, raced to the pen, and leaped the fence. Instantly, there was a whirling mass of teeth and claws. Chickens shrieked and feathers flew.

Suddenly, the intruder leaped the fence, Crust right after him. Skip could get off only one shot before Crust caught up with the enemy. Once again, the terrible fight began.

Boomer came charging out, swinging his gun. "Where is he?" he bellowed. "Lemme get at 'im."

The wolverine wasn't going to be cornered

by two guns and a fiercely fighting dog. Like lightning, he streaked along for cover and disappeared in the undergrowth.

"Dad-blamed thievin' varmint!" Boomer yelled.

Pat arrived on the scene in time to see Crust limp over to Skip. "What's happened?" she cried.

"We just had a little problem with our chickens," Skip answered, keeping his voice calm.

"Little problem!" Boomer exclaimed. "That murderin' varmint! He nailed every one of them good layin' chickens."

Skip couldn't bear to look up at Pat. He knew just how shocked she'd be at this bad news. Instead, he spoke quietly to Crust. "That's a good boy. You're going to be all right."

"I'm glad something's going to be all right," Pat cried out. "All those wonderful chickens — gone!"

In the morning, Toby and Jenny, who'd slept through the night's dreadful excitement, hurried out to join Boomer on his tracking expedition around the lake.

"Are you sure it's a wolverine track?" Toby asked. "Maybe it was that old Scarface."

"Nope. Wolverine, all right. I'd know old Scarface's track. Once you see it you ain't inclined to disremember it."

"How would you know it, Boomer?" Jenny asked.

"If'n it's old Scarface, the track is turned sideways. That's from a broken leg. He got his head and foot caught in a bear trap once. Now, he's the meanest critter in these parts. Meaner'n a grizzly."

Jenny shuddered. "Gosh — I guess you can't blame him. That must have been awful."

"Wal, he's got the Devil's own tattoo on him now," Boomer growled.

Toby, just about to ask for further information on the Devil's tattoo, forgot his question as a giant cracking sound filled the air. A big aspen tree in full autumn colors came crashing toward them.

"Get outta here!" Boomer yelled. He snatched up Toby in one arm and swung Jenny around with the other. The tree missed them by inches, spraying leaves and branches as it thundered to the earth.

"What was *that*!" Jenny gasped.

"Beaver," Boomer answered almost at the moment another aspen boomed down. "We better get outta here," he said. "They's makin' theirselves a dam by the sound of things. We wouldn't want 'em to feel stared at, would we?"

By the time Toby discovered that his arm was bleeding from the raking slash of a fallen branch, they were well out of beaver territory.

"Gosh!" he exclaimed, amazed. "That's the first time I've ever been hurt and didn't even know it."

"I could tear a strip off my shirt," Jenny said worriedly. "That cut should be bandaged."

"Not so fast, young lady." Boomer put his hand over Jenny's before she could rip the blue and white checks. "Just hold on. I saw some woundwort around here not a minute ago."

Toby backed up. "I don't want any warts on me!"

"Maybe it's spelled W-O-R-T," Jenny said. "That's how spiderwort is spelled — with an 'o'."

"Wal, this won't give you no warts no matter how it's spelled," Boomer said. He crushed some leaves and plastered them over the cut. "Soldiers used it in battle to stop bleedin'."

From far away came the sound of the dinner bell at the cabin. "Let's go!" Toby cried, forgetting his arm and remembering his stomach. "Am I *hungry*."

But he was not too hungry to stop outside

the cabin and give his father a thrilling account of how they all had been nearly killed. "By a beaver," he explained. "It sawed a tree down while we were just about standing under it. And then —"

Oddly enough, Skip didn't seem interested in hearing more. "Go wash up, Toby," he interrupted. "Your mother's got dinner about ready."

Toby, disappointed, trotted off with Jenny. "You'd think he'd *want* to hear how we were nearly killed."

Jenny frowned. "I think he doesn't want Mom to hear. We'd better be careful, Toby, or she's apt to say we should go back to L.A."

"Why? We could get killed there, couldn't we?"

"Well, not by a beaver," Jenny replied. "Let's forget it."

On the cabin steps, Boomer paused to give Skip an account of the wolverine's whereabouts. "When them varmints get hungry, they're likely to try anything," he said.

Skip sighed. "Hope you're not trying to scare us, Boomer."

"No, *sir*! Just tryin' to let you know what you might be in for. Since he got the chickens, he's likely to try for somethin' else." He looked at Skip's gloomy face. "Tell you what, Skip — I ain't been a trapper fer nuthin' all these years. I could —"

Skip shook his head. "No traps, Boomer — not with my kids running all over the place."

"Who said anythin' about traps?" Boomer demanded. "What'd ya think I carry a gun fer? Shootin' bean cans? Now this is what I have in mind — there's a sight of work around here. Don't mean no offense, but yore 'guest house' could stand some chinkin'. And the roof fixed a bit steadier. It'd make a great place for Marybelle this winter. And I'd shore enjoy it durin' my stay. How'd it be if we fixed things wolverine-proof, ya might say? Maybe that varmint would plumb give up."

"I couldn't ask you to do all that, Boomer."

The old trapper's eyes twinkled. "No? What if I say I'm fixin' to stick around for your wife's big Thanksgiving dinner? Kinda like to earn my keep, ya know."

Boomer more than "earned his keep." Not only was the old cabin tightened for winter weather, but other "improvements" were made. And, best of all for Jenny and Toby, Boomer knew where to look for the very last wild berries and nuts. His quick eye could also spot the smallest leafy plant, the tiniest paw-print. Soon the Robinson family realized they'd been *looking* but not quite *seeing* all the beauty of their wilderness home.

Glowing jars for future berry pies were soon lined up on Pat's shelves. And Skip was starting what he called "The Boomer Collection of Home Remedies." "Boomer, what you don't know about this country wouldn't fill a book," he said one evening as he worked to neatly label dried roots and crushed leaves.

Jenny looked suprised. "I'd say what Boomer *does* know *would* fill a book."

"Why don't we make one?" Toby asked. "We could call it a good name, like — like — How about *Bouncing Around with Boomer*?"

Boomer looked alarmed. "Hold on! I ain't the bouncin' type."

Jenny frowned. "How about just *Boomer's Book*?"

"No objection," Boomer said calmly. "You can borry my name free."

"Certainly not," Pat said. She put down her knitting and looked off into space. "You know, Toby does have a good idea. Why don't we all pitch in and turn out a small handbook-guide sort of thing? Maybe we'd all become enormously wealthy."

Boomer haw-hawed, "And right off I'd buy me a motorcycle down to Three Forks and go a-bouncin' up and down the mountains. No thank ya, ma'am. Just spell my name right, and that'll do for me."

Thanksgiving Day — and on the Robinsons' dinner table was a feast fit for a king.

Boomer could hardly believe his eyes when he saw the roasted chestnuts, cranberry sauce, fried apples, corn, peas, sweet potatoes, *and* a wonderful golden-brown turkey!

"Where'd you get it?" he gasped, staring at the plump, beautiful bird.

"Heard him gobbling across the lake," Skip grinned.

"And guess what!" Pat exclaimed. "Just about everything else came right from our garden."

"Except the pie insides," Toby added. "They're the berries you helped us find, Boomer."

"Wal, I declare!"

Skip bent his head and gave thanks for the bounty spread before them. Boomer was about to open his eyes when Skip added special thanks: "And thank You for letting Boomer be with us today..."

"*Ah*...men!" Toby exclaimed.

Boomer could hardly trust himself to look up once more at the happy faces around the table. "Wild onions," he said loudly, pushing a small bowl aside. "Never was a time yet that a wild onion couldn't get my eyes to watering!"

4

Boomer had a beautiful morning to start his journey over the ridge. High above the mountain peaks, wind-streaked white clouds swept along against a pale blue sky.

Packed and ready to go, Boomer put his foot on Flora's rump, pulling heavily on the rope holding the pack. Surprised, and slightly displeased by such treatment, Flora grunted her disapproval.

"Which way *exactly* are you going, Boomer?" Toby asked.

Boomer jerked the last knot tight and looked up. He pointed. "See that big, lovely peak over there all proud and beautiful?"

The Robinsons all looked toward the majestic snow-covered range and nodded.

"Well, now — there's a pass 'tween her and the one to the left. I dunno what the maps named her, but I call her 'Leila' 'cause that's a beautiful name, like her."

"She *is* beautiful," Jenny said, making up her mind that in the future she would call all mountains "she" — except for maybe Pike's Peak. "Pike's Peak, she — " just wouldn't sound right.

Toby shuffled his feet. "Well, when you get to the pass, then were do you go?"

"Down over into Elk Creek and do me some trappin' for the winter. Then come spring, I head back to Leila. Mebbe do a little gold-hunting like I been doin' for forty years now." A faraway look came into his eyes. "Every now and then Leila gives me a nugget or two. Who knows? Mebbe she'll say to me next time, 'Boomer, you're gonna strike it rich.' "

Toby's eyes grew round. "I sure'd like to hear a mountain talk to me! Wish I could go with you sometime, Boomer."

"Wal, now. Who knows?" Boomer turned and held out his hand to Skip. "I'll be saying good-bye. Good luck, now."

Pat smiled warmly. "Hurry back, Boomer.

We'll miss you. And you're always welcome here."

Boomer smiled shyly at Pat. "Ma'am, I shore appreciate all 'em fine vittles. You're a mighty fine cook and a gen-u-ine nice lady. You just be thinkin' of me 'bout around dusk-time. I'll be a-dining on yore turkey sand-wiches nice as you please."

Toby and Jenny followed alongside Flora a few steps as Boomer started off. "Hey!" Toby cried. "There he is! It's the eagle again!"

Overhead an eagle soared and dipped low. Boomer grinned. "That's no *he*, that's Clemen-tine! Old Jake — who lived here before ya — he raised her from a nestling, jest like he raised that raccoon and that no-count Samson of yours."

He stretched out his arm and Clementine swooped in for a perfect landing. "She's mighty friendly, all right," Boomer went on. "But you gotta watch her. She gets an ornery streak sometimes."

As though to prove him right, Clementine nipped Boomer's floppy hat right off his head and winged away.

"Dang you, Clementine!" Boomer roared. "You come back here with that hat!"

Clementine made another swoop, dropping

the hat right under Flora's nose. The mule obligingly picked it up and swung her head around to Boomer. "Thank you both," Boomer grinned.

From the cabin porch, Pat and Skip watched as last good-byes were made and the children began to trudge back to the cabin. Suddenly, Toby spun back. He ran, waving his arm. "I love you, Boomer," he shouted.

Boomer waved back, then set his course for his beloved Leila. And this time there were no wild onions to explain the two big tears that welled up in the old trapper's eyes.

By the "dusk-time" Boomer had mentioned, dark clouds were piling up in a blood-red sky. A whistling wind sent dry, dead leaves rattling against the cabin windowpanes. The lonesome cry of a loon didn't help lift Jenny's and Toby's spirits, either. And when Jenny burst into tears over the sight of yesterday's turkey, and said chokingly, "Boomer!" Toby nearly wept, too.

Skip and Pat exchanged glances. Pat nodded slightly and Skip cleared his throat. "Boomer said we'd had a nice long fall, but he expected a big change in the weather any day now."

Neither young Robinson looked up. "And

so," Pat continued, "he suggested that maybe it would be a good idea tonight to put together a surprise he left us."

"Surprise?" Jenny asked, not very cheerfully, and hardly glancing up.

"Where is it?" Toby asked, looking around, interested.

"Out in the guest house. I'll need help bringing it in, so finish your dinner before it's too dark."

"What is it?" Jenny asked, helping herself to sweet potatoes.

"I told you. A surprise."

"Oh, *Daddy*!"

"Eat," Pat smiled. "Looks to me as though I'll be stuck with the dishes tonight in honor of Boomer's surprise."

But doing dishes was not such a bad job — not when she could look over at her family by the fireplace. Bandido and Crust were the only family members not taking part in the activities. They both snoozed on through the thumps of a hammer, the rasping noise of sandpaper smoothing wood to a satin smoothness, and the excited voices of Jenny and Toby as they helped put the finishing touches on Boomer's gift to them all — a wonderful family-size *sled*!

* * *

The Robinsons awoke to a dazzling white world. The first storm of winter had left a foot or more of snow to make a wonderland beyond the cabin door.

"Toby!" Jenny cried. "Come look!"

"Wow! It's like make-believe!" Toby gasped, squeezing past his sister to dip his hands in the powdery fluff.

"And nobody's ever stepped on it." Jenny's voice was hushed. "It's our very own snow!"

After morning chores were done, Marybelle milked, and turkey soup set to simmer for lunch, the Robinsons, Crust, and the two bear cubs trundled out into the snow. Skip set two large dishpans on the sled, and with Crust bounding on ahead, they began the hike to the top of the long, sloping meadow hill.

"What are the dishpans for, Skip?" Pat asked, kicking a pathway through the snow.

"You'll see," he laughed. "So will Clementine up there. She's keeping an eye on Boomer's sled, I guess."

Pat looked up at the soaring eagle, then pointed to the ridge. "And there's another interested viewer. See that deer looking down on us? Those dishpans had better be good! They're going to have quite an audience."

At the top of the hill, Skip handed a dishpan to Jenny. "Try this for size, Jenny. Toby, here's yours. Here, now. Each one of you take a cub."

Squeezed into their silvery round "sleds," and shrieking with excitement, Toby and Jenny waited for the push that would send them spinning and rushing downhill. Crust, not invited to share a dishpan, held no grudge. He cavorted joyously behind the foursome and was right there ready to tumble headlong with them in a pileup at the end of a hair-raising course.

While they all trudged back uphill, Pat and Skip started a snowball fight that sent them sailing and toppling into a huge drift. Shouting and laughing, Skip plowed his way out. Behind him, Pat plopped down and fanned her arms to make an angel-shape in the snow. But Skip was up in time to see Toby and Jenny send the little bears on a solo slide in the dishpans.

Suddenly the pans veered off to the left and the cubs went spinning out of sight down the far slope of the hill. Unseen by the Robinsons, the two furry tobogganners were upended into the side of another snowy slope. Out they spilled — straight onto the ledge that served as a front porch for a very angry female cougar.

The bear cubs didn't wait for her angry second snarl that said "beat it!" They gathered short legs beneath furry bellies and struck out for high ground — and friends.

But Crust's ears had caught that high-pitched sound of fury. Perhaps if he hadn't started to the rescue, the big cat would have been content to spit with contempt at the small, waddling balls of fur. But the sight of the dog plunging down from the crest of the hill changed that. And behind him, legs churning the snow, came Toby.

With an enraged scream, the cougar raced to meet the enemy halfway.

Toby stopped, terrified. "Dad! Dad!" he shouted with all the force he could bring to his cry, "Crust is fighting a cougar!"

Followed by Jenny, Skip raced down the curving snowtrack of the dishpans. Horrified as Toby, he saw the rolling, slashing, snapping sight below. "Get back!" he yelled at Toby.

Twisting, bending, and jerking a low tree branch, Skip broke it free and went tearing off down the slope. Like a swordsman of old, he leaped into the fray, wielding the branch left and right.

As snow flew in all directions, Toby's and Jenny's view was almost blotted out. "Dad-deee!" Toby screamed in terror.

Jenny saw her father's legs shoot out beneath him. Down he went in the very midst of slashing paws and bared fangs. "Get away!" she screamed. "Daddy! Get *away*!"

Skip managed to get the fingers of one hand around Crust's collar. It took all his strength to pull back the plunging dog and at the same time push hard at the furious cougar. With a last screaming snarl and a forward slap of murderous claws, the cougar suddenly called it a day. She wheeled, and ran.

Jenny and Toby rushed down the hill. "Daddy — are you hurt?" Jenny yelled.

"I'm OK," her father panted.

"Boy, Dad!" Toby exclaimed. "I thought you were a goner!"

So did Pat. At the top of the hill she stood immobile as a statue, mittened hand at her throat.

Skip, still keeping a tight hold on Crust, made slow progress back up through the snow. Toby began to run on ahead. Jenny caught up with him and snatched his arm. "Toby, don't say anything dumb like, 'Did you see Dad fight the cougar?' Mom saw it, all right, and she's scared."

Toby stared. "Scared? Why? It's all over and we won."

"L.A.," Jenny muttered. "Remember?"

"L.A.? *Oh!*"

Jenny was right about their mother being upset. She and Toby stayed quiet while Skip begged Pat to calm down.

She burst into tears. "Calm *down.* My — my *family* was almost killed by a wild animal."

Skip put his arm around her. "Pat — we weren't in any real danger."

"No real danger? Then what are those blood stains on the snow? Look at that rip in your jacket. Why, you were practically eaten by that cougar. She could have killed you!"

Skip laughed. "Come on, Pat! Do I look 'practically eaten'? I'm all in one piece."

Jenny patted her mother's arm. "It wasn't Dad's fault," she said earnestly.

Pat jerked her arm away. "Jenny, I'm talking to your father."

Toby and Skip, nearly as shocked and hurt as Jenny, stared at Pat. Jenny was first to speak. Her voice shook. "You've always said we were a *family.* And that what happens to one of us, happens to *all* of us."

Pat did her best to steady her own voice. "Jenny, we'll talk later. Skip, you're probably right. But I — I just want to be alone."

Boomer would have been disappointed if he'd seen his sled's first downhill coast. Pat Robinson wasn't aboard.

By lunchtime the Robinsons were all in better spirits, and by the time dinner was over they were a family again. Crust was gnawing at the bandage Jenny and Toby had insisted he must wear on his leg, and Skip was almost enjoying *his* bandaged shoulder. Pat and Jenny got out their sewing kits and argued over who should mend the hero's torn jacket. Toby put himself in charge of popping corn at the fireplace.

Suddenly the two-way radio crackled. "Hello, Queen Roger Tango Six Three Apple. This is Medic Two. Do you copy...?"

Jenny leaped up. "It's Doctor Mike," she said excitedly.

Pat went to the radio. "Hello Medic Two, this is Six Three Apple. We read you loud and clear. How are you, Mike?"

"Fine, Pat. How's the Robinson family? Everybody well?"

Pat smiled over at Skip. "Couldn't be better," she said. "Skip tangled with a cougar this morning, but he's fine now."

"A *cougar*! *That* doesn't sound too good. Watch for any sign of infection."

Jenny saw an anxious look come into her mother's face. She spoke up hastily. "You should have seen Daddy, Dr. Mike. He was so brave."

"Hey! What are you folks doing up there? It sounds like a shooting match."

"I'm popping corn," Toby called out.

"Wish I had some, Toby. Say, is your dad listening?"

"Hi, Mike. I'm right here."

"Good. Listen, Skip — Would you folks like to make a visit to town before it freezes over up there?"

Jenny bounced up. "Dad, let's go. Please. I want to go Christmas shopping."

"So do I!" Toby yelled.

Pat looked at Skip and smiled. He nodded. "OK, Mike. The motion is carried," he said.

"Good. I'll send Stan out in the morning to pick you up."

Jenny and Toby, excited about the next day's journey, almost forgot to eat the popcorn.

But long after her children were settled down in the loft bunk beds, Pat lay awake. She couldn't forget that for miles and miles beyond her cabin home stretched a wilderness, beautiful — and savage.

5

To the Robinsons, the small town of Three Forks seemed just as busy and booming as a big city. Christmas decorations were everywhere, and store windows filled with wonderful things to buy.

But tucked away in the midst of all these wonderful sights was a sight that brought chills to the hearts of Toby and Jenny — a neat sign right across from Dr. Mike's office: A.J. PERKINS, D.D.S.

Worse yet was the fact that they were going *in*!

For the moment, Toby forgot the joys of Main Street. "I sure don't like city life," he announced to his family. "I thought stuff like this was why we left L.A."

Jenny nodded. "Personally, I'd rather face a — a *wolverine* than a dentist," she whispered to her father.

Fortunately, Dr. Perkins didn't threaten any of the Robinsons with such deadly weapons as dentist drills or hypodermic needles. In fact, after making them a Christmas-wrapped package of toothpaste samples and the latest thing in brushes, Jenny's opinion completely changed. "Your compliments on our teeth were very nice," she said seriously. "If you're ever up our way, do plan to stay at least overnight."

"Yes," Toby added. "And you needn't bring your own toothpaste. We'll have plenty."

Once again on Main Street they decided to divide forces. "How'd it be," Skip asked Pat, "if Toby and I did our shopping, and you and Jenny did yours? We can meet Mike for lunch at The Coffee Cup at noon."

Shopping went fast for each twosome. By twelve o'clock, Toby had new boots, two pairs of heavy mittens and a raccoon-tailed hat. "I sure hope I don't hurt Bandido's feelings, Dad," he said worriedly. "Maybe I should have picked something else."

Skip grinned. "He'll probably take it as a compliment. Don't worry."

Skip settled for a new jacket and just one longing look at a beautiful pair of skis. "Hundred and seventy-five dollars!" he gasped. "Oh, well — I'll just take another look at the *Wilderness Almanac* and try to make my own skis."

Pat had no trouble in making up her mind in choosing a heavy coat with a fur hood. Jenny needed new clothes more than any other member of the family. "I've grown two complete *sizes*," she groaned. "Mom, I guess I'm an awful expense to you and Daddy."

Pat laughed. "It's the price we pay for having a healthy daughter, I guess. And that's not much compared to having an *unhealthy* daughter. Don't worry."

Jenny frowned. "Well, anyhow, right after Christmas, I'm going to get to work on *Boomer's Book*. Remember what he said about 'earning his keep'? I'm going to earn mine."

At twenty past twelve, the Robinsons were still standing in line at The Coffee Cup waiting for a table. "City life," Toby groaned. "This is the part I hate."

After lunch the family regrouped for secret present-shopping.

By four o'clock there wasn't a Robinson who hadn't decided that the wilderness was the place for them. Jenny and Toby had been nearly run down by a car. Sidewalks, slushy and dirty, left their mark on Toby's pants when he was bumped off his feet by a gang of galloping school kids. "Gosh! They nearly creamed me!" he exclaimed in disgust. "Some kids they got around here!"

Jenny helped him to his feet. "They're probably nice after you get to know them. We have to be fair."

"What's fair about that?" Toby asked. He pointed to the sidewalk. "Look at our presents. They're all slush, and the kids didn't even say 'excuse me.'"

"Maybe our motel will be more fun. We can watch TV like we used to," Jenny said hopefully. "Mom will love it. She told me she's going to read in bed now that she has a chance to have electric lights, and she said she's going to simply swim in the bathtub."

"Who wants to swim in a bathtub?" Toby asked scornfully.

"Mom. Come on."

The day in Three Forks ended almost exactly at the same time as a day in the wilderness cabin — even a little bit earlier. Toby and Jenny fell asleep in the midst of a TV program.

Skip had to turn out Pat's reading light. He glanced at his watch. Eight thirty-five. And he was the only Robinson still awake!

A great welcome awaited them at the cabin. Marybelle bleated excitedly in the guest house. Inside the cabin Crust raced from window to window barking his head off. Bandido stood on the top porch step, more dignified than were the bear cubs tumbling down the snowy path to the dock. And it seemed to Pat that even the winter birds in the big tree at the back of the cabin tweeted a welcome.

That evening, with new supplies stowed away and Christmas presents placed safely out of Bandido's reach, Skip got to work on making a pair of skis. Hardly had he begun when there was a loud *thud* on the cabin door. Crust wagged his tail and lazily stood up. "Samson!" Toby cried as the door was given a second hearty wallop. "Could he come in for a little while, Mom?"

"He most certainly may not," his mother said firmly. "I love him dearly, but he's simply too big for this house."

"But he can't stay in the guest house," Jenny pleaded. "He'd make Marybelle nervous."

Samson seemed to understand that everybody loved him. And after accepting the family's hugs and pattings, he lumbered down off the porch in search of a private room of his own.

"We'll help him find a nice cave tomorrow," Skip said. "Maybe he has one already picked out for his winter hibernation."

The weather next day helped Samson make up his mind to leave home until spring. By late afternoon, snow had already begun to pile up and curve in deep drifts along the cabin. And by nighttime, up on the wooded ridge, wolves sent a mournful winter song to ride the sweeping wind. Boomer's promised winter weather was really setting in.

The Robinsons soon discovered that winter brought a whole new set of chores to be done. Just keeping a narrow path clear to Marybelle's quarters was no small job. And moving supplies from the big woodpile to a smaller one on the front porch was another task that made daily life easier.

As Boomer predicted, the lake had begun freezing over — not yet as deep as five feet of ice, but thick enough to make ice fishing necessary. Skip chose his favorite summer fishing spot for chopping a hole and dropping his line. Toby had once guessed the distance as about "three blocks" along the lake shore from their dock.

That was just far enough away and close enough for a good sled ride with Crust, rigged out in a make-shift harness, doing his best to act like an experienced sled dog.

Skip heard Jenny call out, "Mush, Crust. Mush!" Grinning, he pulled up his line and unhooked the eighth good-sized fish of the morning's catch. "You're just in time, kids," he called as they came around a curve of the shore. He held up the string of fish. "Here. Tell your mother to put four of these in the frying pan. The rest can go in the smokehouse."

"Can't we stay and fish, too, Dad?" Jenny asked.

"Yeah. Then we'd have more fish," Toby pointed out.

"Not this time," their father replied. "You go on and tell Mom I'll be up soon — *hungry*."

Jenny put the fish on the sled and Toby packed a snow barrier around the catch to keep it from sliding off. Crust, still enjoying his importance as lead sled dog, trotted off at a brisk pace, Jenny and Toby "mushing" behind him.

Over in the trees a single wolf sniffed the

air. He moved slowly to the edge of the woods lining the shore. Another wolf padded quietly up. Then a third, a fourth, and a fifth. Crust suddenly strained forward, jerking the rope reins from Jenny's hands. Toby glanced back. "Jenny! Hurry!" he cried out. "Wolves!"

Jenny took one terrified look just as Crust swung away from the shore edge. He headed straight back to Skip's fishing hole. It was hard going. Ice gave him a slippery footing and the sled jerked wildly from side to side on the wooden runners. "Run, Crust! Run!" Jenny screamed, panic-stricken. "Daddy! Help us! Help us!"

But the big powerfully-built lead wolf was closing in. Crust skidded and turned. Snarling savagely he leaped forward, ready to do battle with the enemy.

Before Jenny had cried out, Skip was on his way to his children. "The fish!" he shouted. "Throw 'em the fish!"

Almost as Jenny reached for them, the sled lurched, spun, and skidded farther out from the shoreline. To Skip's horror, he heard the sharp crack of ice giving way. In a fraction of a second Crust, the sled, Jenny and Toby, *and the wolves* plunged into freezing water.

It was all Skip could do to keep his balance as

he came on at a dead run. The wolves were the first to struggle out. As Skip skidded closer, yelling and waving his arms, they straggled as fast as they could back to shore.

Jenny, battling to keep afloat, screamed to Toby to snatch and hang on to the bobbing sled. Crust, tangled in the makeshift harness, was trapped in his efforts to climb out.

With cries of "Help, Dad. Help!" ringing in his ears, Skip skidded to a stop and flattened himself along the thinning ice. "Reach, Toby. Reach!" he shouted, crawling as close to the watery hole as he dared.

Clutching his father's mittened hand, Toby felt himself being pulled to safety. "Don't stand, Toby. Crawl!" Skip panted. Next out was Jenny. Last — the sled, with Crust dragging behind it.

Skip, Toby, and Jenny, flat as turtles, pushed fearfully backward away from thin ice. Crust, unable to stand, bellied along beside them.

Half-dragging, half-pushing his nearly frozen children, Skip got them to their feet. He jerked off his coat and bundled it around two pairs of soaked shoulders. "Move!" he ordered. "You gotta keep moving, kids."

Crust, shivering so much he could hardly

put one strong paw in front of another, went shakily forward.

In the cabin, Pat, happily unaware of the dreadful scene at the lake, checked out a lunch menu. "Bandido! Get down from there! Honestly! It's time you became an outdoor raccoon."

Bandido peeked flirtatiously at her behind crossed paws and didn't budge. "Well, OK." Pat laughed. "You can watch. But stay right there! If you're good, maybe Skip will bring you a fish."

She began setting the table — a proceeding Bandido found fascinating. Pat smiled. "What would you say, young man," she said, "if I told you I wouldn't trade you and the cubs and Samson for all the stores in Three Forks? Surprised, huh?"

Bandido made a sudden leap from the cupboard shelf to the front window. He bounded up a chair arm and scrubbed away a peekhole in the frosty pane. "Kids coming?" Pat asked.

She put down the last soup spoon and went to the door to welcome them. "Skip!"

"Get a tub of warm water," he shouted, struggling along up the path. "Kids fell through the ice!"

Pat flew. In the tub it was Saturday night all

over again — except this time Pat and Skip bundled each dripping child in rough towels and rubbed them until skin glowed and warmth once more began to flow along aching bones and stiffened muscles.

Pat handed out fresh flannel pajamas, woolly robes, fleece-lined slippers, and ordered the pair to the fireside.

"And don't just *sit* there," Skip said. "Do push-ups."

"Skip!" their mother cried out, scandalized. "They've had a terrible shock. Push-ups! They should rest."

"Don't worry, Mom," Jenny said, her teeth still chattering. "We can do both."

"Yes," Toby added chatteringly. "We can rest and dry off Crust at the same time. That'll be better'n push-ups."

"Well, *I've* had a terrible shock!" Pat exclaimed. "Why on earth were you children on the ice anyhow? You know it was breaking rules."

Skip spoke up quickly. "Crust just sort of skidded and the sled swung way out."

"Crust was awful brave, Mom," Toby said. "He was running as hard as he could so's — " Jenny squeezed her brother's arm. "So's we could have a good ride," he said quickly.

Pat's eyes hadn't missed that arm-squeeze. "What was so brave about that?" she asked slowly.

Skip began fussing with his bootlaces. "Well, Pat — as a matter of fact, he was trying to get the fish I caught home as fast as possible."

Pat looked at him steadily. "Oh, that *was* brave! I suppose he was scared to death that they'd spoil in all this hot weather we're having, so he hurried. Now what happened? Or am I the one member of this family who's not supposed to know what goes on around here?"

"It just sounds worse than it was," Jenny lied. "You see, Mom — there was this wolf. He smelled the fish, I guess, Daddy yelled 'throw them the fish,' and — "

" 'Them'?" Pat looked stern. "This story gets better all the time."

"Oh, it does!" Toby said earnestly. "There were five wolves and I counted 'em. And they could have eaten us instead of the fish. But they didn't want to."

Pat dropped down into a chair. "That *is* a happy ending," she said weakly. "Skip, empty the washtub, will you, please? I'll get lunch. *Somebody* has to do something normal around here."

59

That night, long after Jenny and Toby were asleep in the loft, Pat sat staring into the fireplace, her knitting on her lap.

Skip looked across at her. "Hey, now. I know what you're thinking. Sure, there are problems out here. But there are problems anywhere — even in Three Forks."

Pat nodded. "Of course. You're right. It's just that — well, I guess problems look bigger when you don't feel good."

"You don't?" he asked anxiously. "Did you tell Mike McCord?"

"Nothing to tell. I *felt* good — yesterday." She suddenly smiled. "Maybe it's just a touch of wolf-itis. I'll get over it."

It was a good thing for Pat's "touch of wolf-itis" that she was by a snug fireside. Out on the windswept hillside far from the warm, glowing cabin, a wolf pack milled around in search of food. A sudden squabble broke out. Just as suddenly it was brought to an end by the pack leader. Huge, fang-snapping, old Scarface was back in the wilderness valley.

Morning brought crystal-clear skies and howling, swirling winds. Foot-long icicles hung from the cabin roof. Inside, Skip's freshly-laid fire was just beginning to take the

The family cabin looks warm and inviting in the beautiful and savage mountain wilderness.

The Robinson family: Skip, Jenny, Toby, and Pat.

Toby and Jenny play with another family member: the bear cub.

Skip chops the last of the winter wood, the only fuel for the long, cold days ahead.

Boomer arrives for his Thanksgiving visit.

Boomer demonstrates the art of milking Marybelle.

Bandido, the pesky family raccoon, happily greets his old friend, Boomer.

Samson and Boomer clowning around make a funny pair

Boomer stretches out his arm and Clementine swoops in for a perfect landing.

Toby and Skip set out on snowshoes on their day-long hunting trip, and   Crust tags along.

Crust, enjoying his importance as lead sled dog, dashes off at a brisk pace, Jenny and Toby "mushing" behind him.

Skip finds himself in the midst of the wolves' slashing paws and bared fangs.

Clutching his father's coat, Toby feels himself being pulled to safety as Jenny struggles to stay afloat in the icy hole.

Toby thaws out in a warm tub after their frightening ordeal while Pat watches worriedly.

The Robinsons sled down a hair-raising slope in Boomer's handmade toboggan.

With a last screaming snarl, the cougar wheels and runs.

chill off the room. Even Bandido felt like sleeping a bit longer than usual. He stalked over the blankets searching for a cozier spot for another nap. Pat blinked sleepily at him and pulled the covers up over her head.

"All right, sleepyheads!" Skip called out. "Everybody out of bed."

Pat peeked out, yawned, and disappeared again. From the loft came the sound of sneezes.

"Hey, everybody! What is this?" Skip called again loudly. "Is this family waiting for breakfast in bed?"

Toby appeared, bundled up in his bathrobe. "Hey, Mom. My throat's sore," he called down.

Pat was out of bed in an instant. Moments later she called down a report to Skip. "One member of this family *is* having breakfast in bed."

"I'm not sick," Toby protested.

"A sore throat and a warm forehead spells S-I-C-K. Back to bed!"

6

To Pat's relief, there was no need to get on the two-way radio to ask for Dr. Mike's help. Toby's sore throat turned out to be no more than a symptom of a plain, garden-variety cold. His temperature soon came down, and after three days in the loft, he was allowed to join the human race once more.

To his disgust, this privilege extended only to the inside of the cabin. Even worse, Pat decided that he could recover just as well with a school book propped in front of his red nose.

"I never heard of a sick child being *forced* to study," he said crossly.

"Well, I never heard of a sick child being

allowed out of bed," his mother said heartlessly. "By all means, go back to bed, Toby, if you don't feel up to social studies."

"And for goodness sake get *better*," Jenny said. "I've been going to school for three days!"

Pat grinned. "Cheer up! Christmas vacation is just around the corner."

It was really not such a bad week. By Friday, Jenny and Toby had a secret project ready to unveil — a good-sized piece of masonite board left over from Skip's summer carpentry work. In large yellow crayon letters was printed, *The Robinson Map*.

"It's a pictograph," Toby explained. "That's what they call a map with pictures. We were going to wait for Christmas to give it to you, but not much has happened this week."

It certainly had pictures. A mountain peak arose in one top corner. It was labeled "Boomer's Leila." On the lake area was "Stan Coble's seaplane," a figure on the dock was marked "Dr. Mike McCord." And along the shoreline was an upside-down canoe with Crust's head appearing in a circle of ripples.

"We've included adventures," Toby said. "There's one by the smokehouse, and there's another where Dad's ice-fishing."

"And see that arrow?" asked Jenny. " '20

miles to neighbor, 60 miles to Three Forks.' "

Boomer, Flora, Marybelle were shown, as well as a rather large bean can nailed to a small tree. Samson, the cubs, and Bandido were also featured.

Skip and Pat noticed two "adventures" did not appear — a cougar and a wolfpack, although there were eight blobs by the smokehouse labeled "dead chickens."

"It's handsome!" Skip exclaimed. "And I like the way you showed the smokehouse adventure. It tells the whole story."

Toby beamed. "I thought of that myself. Jenny wanted to make a wolverine."

"But I couldn't," his sister said honestly. "I've never seen one up close."

Pat gulped. "I hope you never will!" Quickly, she added, "I like best the way you've drawn the cabin with us all sitting on the porch steps. Really nice."

"Where'll we hang it?" Toby asked. "How about on the front door, Dad? That way you'd see it every time you went out."

"And it would be handy for adding any new stuff that happens," Jenny agreed.

Their mother jumped up. "My goodness! I smell the pies. I certainly hope the crusts aren't too brown." She hurried away to the stove.

Skip sniffed the air. *He* didn't smell pies burning. But it was a very handy reason for Pat's leaving it up to him as to where the gift should be placed. *Not* on the door — he was sure of that. He knew Pat dreaded the children's adding even one more "adventure" to their map.

"Hmm. How about leaning it over there against the wall?" he asked. "That way it would be easier to move around and work on when you want to."

It was agreed.

One week was almost too much resting time for Toby to sleep as soundly as the rest of the family that night.

Shrieking winds buffeted the corners of the loft. "Boy, I'm glad I'm not out there now. Poor Marybelle. I wonder if she's scared."

As though in answer, a faint maa-aa-ing bleat reached his ears. He sat up, listening. Another blast of wind snatched at the walls, drowning out all other sounds. Toby snuggled back. "Guess I imagined it," he muttered.

But Marybelle *was* scared, even though she was safe behind the walls Boomer had carefully tightened. *Something* was outside. Something sinister and prowling. And Marybelle knew it.

Although a brilliant moon shone down on the white-blanketed lake and hillside, it made the shadows even deeper. And in the black shadow of the smokehouse, a killer was abroad.

The wolverine snuffled around to the snow-drifted doorway of the smokehouse and clawed at the frame. The wooden latch was the next thing to explore. Even though banked snow put it closer to the wolverine's reach, the small animal had to leap upward for an experimental bite. Again and again it jumped and each time its vicious teeth closed down and jerked at the fastening.

The wolverine was not the only forest creature driven by hunger. In the moonlight, six wolves moved single file down the long slope from the ridge. Clouds of windblown snowflakes hid the raiders from sight as old Scarface, leading the pack, headed toward the Robinson smokehouse. In the moonlight, his big gaunt frame moved along, silent and sinister, fast closing the distance between the pack and the wolverine.

At the smokehouse door, the wolverine made a last triumphant leap. Down came the last plug of wood, as a blast of wind swung the door wide open.

In a frenzy of excitement the wolverine sniffed the hanging haunches of venison, moosemeat, and smaller game set aside for winter food supply. Swiftly he went inside.

The howl of the wind masked the wolves' approach. The wolverine, so close to the banquet before him, failed to catch their scent. But a terrified bleat from Marybelle announced their arrival. And this time Toby *knew* it. In the moonlit cabin he scurried down the loft ladder and over to Skip's bed. "Dad," he whispered. "Dad."

Skip awoke instantly. "What...what's wrong, Toby?"

"Something's going on outside."

Skip flopped back on his pillow. "Wind. Go to bed, Toby."

"But Crust knows, Dad. He's growling. And I heard Marybelle."

Now really awake, Skip reached for his clothes and boots.

Out in the smokehouse a massacre was going on. Snarls, yelps, growls mingled in the howling wind and swirling snow — a fighting wolverine was losing to the jaws and lean, muscled bodies of gaunt wolves. He didn't stand a chance. No sooner had he ripped at one than two more took its place. Still, the small animal fought on. It was Scarface who put an end to it all. Matching the wolverine in sheer ferocity he went straight for the smaller animal, muzzle pulled back, fangs flashing.

With a despairing angry leap, the wolverine streaked out the door, Scarface at his heels. Only when the wolverine made it to the safety of the brushy growth beyond the smokehouse did Scarface call it off. With one last snarl, he turned and joined the pack in its snapping, crunching, ripping feast.

On the cabin porch, Skip held tight to Crust's collar. The screaming wind wiped out the sound of Crust's growls. And although Skip listened intently, not a hint of what was happening at the smokehouse reached his ears. Behind him, Toby peeked from the narrowly opened door. Wind. Just wind. Marybelle must have settled down. If it hadn't been for Crust's behavior, Toby would have thought he'd dreamed the whole thing.

After breakfast, Skip stepped out to milk Marybelle and fork hay into her special feed bin. He noted with satisfaction that the cabin roof was clear of snow. "Wind's good for something," he muttered. And thinking of last night's gale reminded him of his venture out on the porch. Frowning, he looked toward the smokehouse. *The door was open*. Marybelle forgotten, he strode over.

There was almost no need to look inside. Churned-up snow, a few clear pawprints, glistening bones, some with scraps of dark red tissue still clinging to them, told the story plainly — even to sorting out one set of wolverine prints and that print Boomer had said he'd never "disremember." Sick with dismay, Skip stepped inside. Not a piece of meat was left. Hours of tracking, skinning, dressing-out, hauling, and finally smoking — and now this!

Grimly, Skip headed once again for Marybelle's quarters. At least there'd be a little milk to hand Pat before he gave her the bad news that the Robinsons were facing months of cruel winter on severely rationed canned provisions.

As their father came into the cabin, Jenny and Toby were just about to leave for a little snowshoe practice. Their mother, putting together a meat loaf, looked up as Skip closed the door.

"Skip, I should have asked you yesterday to bring in some venison. We have enough on hand, but this family will be eating meat loaf until we've thawed out supplies."

"Thaw out supplies! We don't have supplies." Grimly, and in the fewest words possible, he gave them the bad news.

There was no use in trying to put on a cheerful face. The situation was much too serious and they all knew it.

"What are we going to *do* ?" Pat asked unsteadily.

Skip strode over to the wall. He took down his rifle. "You're going to stretch out that meat loaf, honey. And I'm going hunting."

Toby picked up his snowshoes. "I'll help, Dad."

"No, Toby. Not this time."

"But you've taught me to shoot," Toby coaxed. "Boomer said I was good, too. He'd let me go!"

Skip hesitated. "Well, OK. I can use help, I guess."

"Skip," Pat cried. "Don't take him!"

He put his hand on Pat's shoulder. "He'll be OK, Pat. We'll be back well before dark. Got a sandwich or two we could take?"

Silently, she turned away as Skip flipped on the radio.

"... There's a report near Mission Ridge that two head of cattle were killed by a pack of hungry wolves," the announcer said. "George

Benchley, who shot at the wolves, confirmed that the pack was led by a large, black wolf named old Scarface, last reported seen in the bad winter two years ago. First time he's shown up since."

Skip decided to keep it to himself that old Scarface had paid the Robinsons a visit, too. Boomer's description had made that particular wolf much too scary for Pat to hear about now. He flipped the radio off.

With sandwiches in Skip's pack, Crust at their heels, and promises to be careful, the two hunters started off.

After two hours of trudging along on deep powder snow, Toby began to stumble.

"You OK?" his father asked.

Toby nodded. "But I know one thing, Dad. I'd hate to be a snowshoe rabbit. These things make me trip."

Skip, though he pushed along easily on his own snowshoes, was no happier than Toby. "I'd like to *see* at least a snowshoe rabbit. I'm afraid we're out of luck, Toby. I don't think there's a moose or elk left in the mountains." He stopped and looked around over the vast landscape. "We'll just have to keep looking, though, for *something* to put on our dinner table."

Another hour went by before Toby came to a panting halt. "Dad — I'm sorry, but I'm *tired*. Boy!"

Skip stopped. "I can believe it. So'm I," he panted.

"Hey! Look over there at Crust! He's found something!" Toby cried.

Crust certainly had found something. Wolf tracks!

Skip looked at them and frowned. "Maybe they're on the scent of something. Come on, Toby. We'll follow and find out. This may be it!"

At the top of a knoll Skip and Toby had a sudden and clear view of a wilderness tragedy. In the deep snow below, a huge, antlered bull elk struggled belly-deep in that winter death trap. Scarcely able to move, he wasn't going to stand a chance with the wolf pack circling and snapping around him.

"Are they going to kill him, Dad?" Toby whispered.

"Yes...he's trapped."

"Couldn't you shoot and scare away the wolves?"

Skip hesitated. "Son, that elk would never survive the winter even if we could drive off the pack." Slowly, he shook his head. "No,

Toby. Those wolves are hungry. So are we."
He raised the rifle to his shoulder.

"What're you going to do?"

The answer was a rifle shot that echoed
through the high mountain basin. The wolves
scattered. The elk dropped. For a second Toby
covered his eyes. "I didn't know hunting would
be like *this*. Gosh, Dad. That elk was no more'n
a bean can."

Skip looked grim. "It was the wolves or us,
Toby. And that elk means —"

His words were lost in a thunderous, roaring *crack* that echoed from mountain to mountain.

"What was *that*?" Toby cried.

"An avalanche somewhere. The shot must
have started it. I didn't think they happened in
such cold weather — only after a spring thaw.
At least it's far away."

"We should have asked Boomer. He'd
know."

"Well, *we* know now, don't we?" Skip
started forward. "Come on. We've got to get
that elk before the wolves come back."

By the time Skip had cut out the meatiest
parts and stowed them in the pack strapped to
his back, he was almost as tired as Toby. And
Toby, carrying the rifle, was not only tired,

but gloomily wondering if he really wanted to be a hunter. Until now, he'd thought of the smokehouse as being a kind of private supermarket; he hadn't connected those hanging haunches with once-living creatures. But he kept his thoughts to himself and paced along, trying to keep up with his father.

Suddenly all thoughts of the killing of the elk vanished. His eyes caught a movement in the undergrowth of the snowy fir trees. He looked again. "Daddy," he called softly, "there's a black wolf following us."

Skip didn't turn his head. "I know. Just keep on going as though you don't notice."

"Is it old Scarface?"

"Don't know," Skip answered. "Just do as I say. Keep going!"

It was hard, tiring, and now frightening work to glide one leg ahead of the other. And Toby couldn't help stealing worried glances at the big, gaunt tracker almost alongside them.

"He's getting closer, Dad!"

"We're OK, Toby. Just relax. We're almost home."

But it was Skip who suddenly stopped walking. "Here. Hand me the gun, Toby."

Toby pulled back. "No, Dad. Don't shoot him! He's just hungry like we'd be if he'd got the elk."

Skip nodded. "I'll just scare him off, Toby."

"Let me do it," Toby pleaded. He swung toward the wolf, lifting the rifle.

Pat and Jenny both heard Toby's rifle shot. "They got something!" Jenny exclaimed delightedly, looking up from the game of checkers they were playing. "Gosh! They've been gone long enough!"

Pat tried to sound surprised. "It seemed long to you? Seems to me this day has just been flying by!" She jumped a black checker over two reds.

"Mother! Pay attention! *I'm* black. You're red."

Pat stood up. "How about putting on our coats and meeting them?"

"Great idea." Jenny giggled. "I'll bet if Toby shot anything we'll never stop hearing about it."

The exploding shot had knocked Toby off his feet. The big animal had loped off a distance, then stopped. Skip grabbed at Crust's collar. "You OK, son?" Skip asked, helping Toby up.

"OK. Dad — it didn't scare him. He's still there."

"I know. But come on. We'll be home soon. He'll go back to the carcass."

But old Scarface didn't turn back. Not yet. Hidden in the brush, he watched, hate in his eyes, as below him Skip waved a tired greeting to the welcoming committee. "Bring the sled!" he shouted cheerfully. "My back's breaking!"

Toby, too tired to even lift his hand, said nothing.

7

In between the return of the hunting expedition and Christmas Eve, the Robinsons each took turns daily at fishing through the now deep-frozen lake. It was not long before the repaired smokehouse provided a ready supply of delicious trout.

"I'm afraid there'll be no Christmas turkey tomorrow, Pat," Skip said, tossing a bit of fish over in the snow for Bandido. The cubs tumbled up for their share.

"Don't worry," Pat laughed. "Fish is the preferred menu around here — at least where a raccoon and bears are concerned. And we're having a roast."

"Make it a small one," Skip said. "I won't feel easy about that elk meat getting used up until we have venison hanging in the smokehouse."

"Will you take Toby next time? I haven't heard him say one word about wanting to go."

"Sure, I'll take him. It's that or not sharing meat at the table."

"Skip! You *wouldn't*."

Skip put down his knife. "I would. I'm glad he's got it out of his head that hunting's fun. What he has to get *in* his head is that when hunting is necessary — he hunts. Just like his old man."

Jenny came around the corner of the cabin. "Are we going to get our Christmas tree today?" she called. "Toby and I picked out one that's just beautiful."

Her father laughed. "Sure — if it's a beautiful one close by. Go get the sled and we'll get it now."

In the leaping light and shadow cast by the glowing fireplace, the Robinson tree did look beautiful. Even the dough angel Pat had made and the children had painted seemed pleased with the view from the top of the tree.

Jenny was just about to tie on the last of the white dough stars and snowflakes when there was a loud thumping on the cabin door.

"My goodness!" Pat exclaimed, startled. "Samson's come out of hibernation! Oh, dear!"

Cautiously, Skip opened the door a crack.

"Ho! Ho! Ho!"

"Boomer!" Toby shouted. "Boomer! You've come back!"

"Just in time for *Christmas!*" Jenny squealed.

Boomer's eyes twinkled. "Christmas! Now who'd a-guessed it was Christmas time? Me — I just happened to be passin' through. Changed my mind since I last seen ya and went down to Three Forks. Found old Flora a nice cozy stable down thataway and I thought I'd drop by here before headin' back to my trapping ground. Reminds me — " He held out a big sack to Pat. "Fer the family, ma'am."

"A goose!" Pat cried, looking into the sack. "Skip! Goose for Christmas! This is *wonderful.*"

"Where on earth did you get it, Boomer?" Skip asked.

"Ran smack dab into me," Boomer grinned. "And, say, Toby — I got a little something fer you, too." He pulled out a handsome hunting knife. "Comes in handy when yore skinnin' a hide."

"Gosh, Boomer!" Toby hesitated.

"Go ahead. Keep it. It's yourn." Grinning, he reached into his pack and pulled out a pair of fur slippers. "These'll keep your toes warm, Jenny."

Jenny and Toby looked at each other. "I'll get it," Toby said. "Don't you tell him what it is, Jenny." He dashed off up to the loft.

"It won't be wrapped right for Christmas," Jenny explained. "We didn't know you'd be here. But it's wrapped."

"Pshaw!" Boomer reddened with pleasure.

Pat and Skip nearly gasped aloud when Boomer lifted his gift from white tissue paper.

"It's personally autographed," Toby said eagerly, as Boomer opened out the folded leather case.

"Well, *now*!" Boomer gulped. "If this ain't a real surprise."

It certainly was! Pat's own desk picture back in L.A. days of her two children! She felt Toby's hand close suddenly on hers. "You got *us*, Mom," he whispered quickly.

Boomer shook his head. "If this don't beat

all! You kids didn't have to go do somethin' like this!"

"I think they did, Boomer," Pat said smiling. "You're their best friend."

"Merry Christmas!" Jenny and Toby cried out. "*Everybody*!"

Boomer finished his last bite of pie. He groaned loudly. "Well, now, that's gotta be the finest Christmas dinner I ever ate."

"It was certainly the finest goose *I* ever ate," Pat laughed.

Jenny looked around the table, her face glowing. "Hasn't this been wonderful? I wouldn't trade places with anybody."

"Me, neither!" Toby exclaimed.

Suddenly the radio crackled. As though to make the day complete, Dr. Mike McCord sent Christmas greetings from Three Forks. "And don't forget," he said. "If you need us up there for anything, just holler! Merry Christmas, everyone!"

Best of all, Boomer promised to stay until the day after New Year's. Even though Toby and Jenny urged Boomer to share their loft, Boomer refused. "Marybelle and me's old friends," he winked. "And she's right perfume-y."

It was a perfect Christmas!

During the holiday week, Boomer, with Skip's help, showed the children how to build a snowhouse.

"First you pick out a nice size snowdrift," he said. "You dig in a bit, and then another bit, and first thing you know, you got a snug little snowroom to keep you outen' the cold."

"But snow's cold," Jenny objected. "How could snow keep you warm?"

Boomer pushed back his floppy hat and scratched his head. "Seems queer, don't it? But it works. The snow acts just like a blanket. It keeps cold out and keeps all the warm feeling you got in."

"Like how Samson keeps warm when he's hibernating, I guess," Toby nodded. "I understand."

But Boomer didn't understand the fun of ice skating on their lake. After the first spill he said so. "Now why should a fella like me care to bust his bottom?" he asked the entire family. "Been avoidin' icy places all my life."

He looked over the space the family had swept clear for an ice rink. "Tell you what — you folks just keep on with your fancy shenanigans. I'm going up to Marybelle's cottage and build you a surprise."

The surprise turned out to be a V-shape snowplow. "You can hitch Crust to it," Boomer explained, "and save yoreselves a sight of work. Be a good idea for makin' a path 'twixt Marybelle and yore residence, too."

New Year's Eve in the wilderness was the most beautiful of all beautiful wilderness nights. Bright moonlight turned the snow-blanketed world into a thousand silvery crystal shapes on the frozen surfaces of the forest and slopes.

"Look at those stars, Skip." Pat waved her arms toward the sky. "Millions. It's just a fairyland! Why don't we go back to the cabin and ask Boomer and the children to come out with us? This is too beautiful to miss."

Skip hugged her. "OK. I guess it's about half-an-hour to midnight."

Pat snuggled her fur hood beneath his chin. "Happy New Year right now!" she exclaimed happily.

"Happy New Year!" he laughed.

Pat looked up. "It'll be a good year ahead, Skip. I know it. It'll be a good year for all of us."

Boomer could not be tempted to give up his comfortable place by the fireside for a wilderness stroll. "Believe I'll just sit here and keep the fire burnin' while you young'uns go gallivantin'." He yawned.

"Don't you go to sleep, Boomer," Jenny warned. "We're all going to sing 'Should Auld Acquaintance be Forgot' exactly at midnight!"

In the huge silence of the wilderness night, the Robinsons looked at the glistening mountain peaks cupping around their very own home. The lake, the slopes, the forest, the starry sky — yes, it would be a wonderful year ahead!

"I *love* this place!" Jenny said softly. "Mom, thank you and Dad for bringing me here."

"Look!" Toby whispered. "There's an otter. See him? He's sliding down the snowbank. I'll bet he's the same one that made us tip over the canoe."

"If it is, it isn't bothering his conscience," Pat chuckled. "He's really celebrating!"

The small creature didn't stop his frolicking as the family headed back to the cabin. Merrily he slid down, climbed up, and repeated the performance. "Happy New Year, otter," Toby cried out.

"Happy New Year!" the rest of the family called.

Nobody sang "Auld Lang Syne" with more gusto than Boomer, even though he had just been awakened from a sound nap. Even Bandido and the bear cubs were impressed. "Look at our music lovers," Skip laughed. "Boomer, you've got them spellbound!"

Boomer cackled heartily. "Got myself kinda spellbound. Ain't greeted a New Year since I don't know when." His voice took on an extra-deep boom. "Happy New Year, Robinsons! And many of 'em!"

8

True to her word, Pat started "school" the day Boomer left. "No use sitting around being lonesome," she said firmly, getting out the books. "Boomer's work is trapping and *he's* started off doing it. Your work is school. Toby, cheer up. The world hasn't come to an end."

"But Boomer likes his work," Toby said gloomily. "It's different when you like what you're s'posed to do."

"You wouldn't like what he does, Toby," Jenny said promptly. "You don't even like hunting."

"Who says?" Toby demanded.

"Well, I haven't heard you begging Daddy to take you."

Pat thumped down notebooks. "There's one thing *I* don't like, and that's bickering," she said sharply.

Both Toby and Jenny stared in surprise. "We're just talking, Mom," Jenny said.

"Same as usual," Toby added.

Their mother sighed. "I guess you're right, Toby. But we're going to have to be extra careful about — well, bickering. You see, we've a lot of winter still ahead and — and we don't want to get on each other's nerves."

"Sure, Mom," Toby agreed. "All we got is us. We know that."

"And I like Toby a lot," Jenny said.

Toby looked surprised. "You *do*?"

"Sure." Jenny reached for the stacked books. "What are we going to start on first?"

"Math," Toby answered.

"OK." Jenny pulled out her math text book. "I will too, then." She grinned at her mother. "I'll do it while my brain's fresh. It's apt to get tired in a hurry when I do math."

"I'll help you if you get stuck," Toby said grandly.

"OK. And I'll help you with spelling."

That morning was not to be the last of the times their mother would speak in an unexpectedly sharp way. As the days went by,

Jenny and Toby found it was harder and harder to "just talk," and easier and easier to "bicker." Winter storms kept them almost snowbound. Their father even strung a rope between the cabin and Marybelle's quarters, "just to make sure nobody gets lost going back and forth out there," he'd said.

But weather changes were swift. On bright, beautiful days the whole family would put aside all but the most necessary chores to build snowmen, go sledding, have snowball fights, have snowshoe races, or try out the pairs of skiis Skip had made for each of them. And winter slowly edged closer to spring.

On one such beautiful morning, Pat decided a necessary chore was the family washing. Outdoors, Jenny and Toby lifted the washtubs to the metal-frame bench their father had made from pipes flown up in the summer from Three Forks. When they'd filled each tub with snow, Skip started a blazing fire beneath the bench.

Pat came out, her arms loaded with sheets and pillowcases. "Isn't this a wonderful way to do a washing?" she asked. "Think of all those poor city folks cooped up in laundromats!"

Skip squinted in the bright sunshine. "I think I'll bring out Marybelle. She'd enjoy a little airing."

As he started away, Pat turned smiling to Jenny and Toby. "I can manage this. Why don't you two take a holiday? You have your teacher's permission."

"What'll we do?" Jenny asked. "Gosh, Mom — we've already done everything a million times."

Pat's smile vanished. "For goodness sake! *Think* of something!" she retorted.

Jenny took a quick look at Toby and he looked as quickly toward her. They hurried off around to the front of the cabin. "It's one of those get-mad-quick days," Toby sighed. "Well, what'll we do?"

"We could go maple-syruping," Jenny suggested. "Maybe the sap is beginning to run."

"Not this early," Toby replied. "When Dad nailed up the pails he said —"

"Oh, for goodness sake, silly! The whole idea is to *do* something, isn't it? Anyhow, we won't know if we don't look. We could go to the edge of the woods and check pails around there. Mom would be *delighted* if we brought some home."

As there was a strict rule that the edge of the woods was the play boundary, Toby couldn't make any real objection. Besides, he didn't care to be called "silly." Though he did think Jenny was silly to look for sap so early in the year.

"OK," he agreed. "What do we use for pails *in case* we find anything?"

"The berry pails. What else?"

It was past noon before Pat and Skip came in from outdoors. "Where're the kids?" Skip asked.

"Oh, I told them to call it a holiday," she answered gaily. "They're outside somewhere."

Skip flipped on the radio just in time to hear the last of the noonday report. "The weatherman says another storm is brewing up. So you folks up north of us better dig in for a big snowfall."

He glanced out the window. Over in the west the skies were heavy with clouds but sunshine was still making a glare of white on the snowbound lake. He sighed. "If it weren't for Marybelle's 'perfume-y' personality, I'd bring her in here. It'd save plowing out in the morning to milk her."

Pat laughed and bent over the stove. "Skip Robinson — the day we live with a goat is the day I'm packing up!" She looked over at him, smiling. "Why don't you ring the dinner bell? Everything will be ready by the time the children are back."

It was the last time that day Pat Robinson smiled.

At least an hour earlier, Jenny and Toby discovered that the pails their father had fastened to the trees nearest the forest edge held nothing but snow. Jenny eyed the trees farther up the hill. "Let's take a quick look up there."

Toby pointed up to the left. "Dad nailed them over that way. I remember."

"OK. Let's look."

Off they went, expertly clopping uphill on their snowshoes.

"I was *sure* they were around here," said Jenny, when they reached the top. "Maybe they were just down the other side."

"It was off to the left," Toby insisted. "I remember. We kept walking sort of at an angle."

By the time Skip pulled on the dinner bell, Jenny and Toby, on the far side of the hill, were out of earshot. And Jenny and Toby were lost!

When the first flakes of snow drifted lazily down, Toby's stomach had already been telling him for a good two hours that lunchtime was long past. "This is your fault," he said angrily. "Who ever heard of sap running when it's still snowstorm time?"

"You kept saying, 'No, over to the left,' " Jenny retorted. "I shouldn't have listened to you!"

"Well, I shouldn't have listened to you," Toby exploded.

But as the wintry afternoon shaded down to deep gray skies and fat snowflakes turned to driving ice crystals, quarreling was forgotten.

"I — I don't know how I got so mixed up," Jenny said, keeping a mittened hand tight over Toby's.

Toby might have said, "Never mind — it's just that it's hard to tell which hill is which." But he didn't. He fought back tears. "Mom and Dad are sure going to have fits! What're we going to do, Jenny?"

Jenny turned her back to the biting wind. "Build a snowhouse," she replied, slowly brushing snow off her eyelashes.

Toby brightened. "OK. We can use the berry pails for shoveling."

"Great idea! First we find a snowdrift."

"That'll be easy," Toby said dismally.

"We'd better hurry. It's snowing harder every minute."

It was real work, and by the time they had hollowed out a space big enough to huddle in, each was steamy warm from exercise. They snuggled in, Jenny holding Toby close. "You OK?"

"I think so," he replied in a small voice. "But what happens if we get all drifted over, Jenny?"

"Don't worry," Jenny said stoutly. "Dad and Crust will find us. You know Crust. He can find *anything*."

"They *can't* find us in the dark. If you hadn't —"

Jenny interrupted angrily. "That's right. Blame everything on me! Nobody *made* you follow me. Besides, you said —"

Toby waved a mittened hand. "Don't *bicker!*"

After that, only the *hiss* of driving snow sifting higher and higher at the snowhouse opening broke the silence of Jenny and Toby's shelter.

Skip, carrying a pack and a rifle, came to a panting halt. Not a single reddening bar of sunlight signaled sunset time. It would soon be dark. Crust looked up at him uneasily, wanting to keep on the move. "Jenny! Toby!" The call echoed and re-echoed. No longed-for cries came back. "Come on, Crust. We'll just have to keep going."

Man and dog stumbled deeper into the forest. Once again Skip stopped — this time to fire the rifle into the air. By now the snow swirled so thick that even if his children were only five feet away Skip wouldn't be able to see them. Tiredly, he slung off the backpack and, taking up his hatchet, began chopping a few fir branches to form a lean-to shelter for himself and Crust. "No use, boy. We'll have to wait 'til dawn."

Crust answered — a sympathetic worried whine that said exactly what Skip was thinking. This was the first night in Crust's life that the Robinsons were not sharing one snug roof.

When Jenny and Toby awoke in the snowhouse, they had no idea if it was dinnertime, midnight, or dawn.

"Maybe it's tomorrow," Toby spoke in the dark. "If it is, we didn't say our prayers last night."

"I did," Jenny said.

"Well, you didn't tell me!"

"I said it for both of us. Say, Toby, do you notice something?"

"Notice something! Who could notice anything in here?"

"I mean *feel*. I'm not as cold as before."

Toby wriggled. "Yeah. Maybe we won't

freeze after all." He suddenly clutched Jenny's arm. "What's that noise?" he asked, his voice dropping low.

Jenny listened. *"Something's trying to get in,"* she answered in a scared whisper.

In the dawn light, a pale, exhausted Pat stirred up the dying fire and placed fresh kindling on it. "If Skip isn't back by noon, I'll get on the radio to Mike," she muttered. "But he *will* be back and he'll have the children. And everybody will be hungry."

Then, as though she were back in L.A. expecting company to drop in any minute, she flew to the stove. "Now what do I have on hand? Let me see. Soup makings. That would be good. They all love soup."

As the sun rose, Pat Robinson was frantically peeling vegetables as though her life depended on making soup.

In his way, Skip was just as frightened. In the pearly dawn light he trudged on, shouting himself hoarse. "Jenny! Toby!"

But two Robinsons, clutching tight to each other in the snowhouse, were beyond plain fright or worry. Paralyzed with fear, they heard the snuffling, growling sounds become louder and louder just beyond the snow wall.

Jenny felt a hard scraping push against her boot. "Hit, Toby!" she screamed. "Bang your boots!" With all her strength she shoved her own boots down hard on the threatening nailed paws. "Go away!" she screamed at the top of her voice. For a second only, the attack worked. The animals backed off. But it was a losing battle. Snow flew. Gray light showed, and ugly, throaty growls seemed almost in their ears. And as a dark, fanged muzzle poked through the broken barrier, Jenny, screaming, flung herself over Toby.

She never heard the rifle shot or Crust's barking or her father yelling, "Jenny! Toby! Jenny! Toby!" She never stopped screaming until a strong hand on her arm pulled her forward. "Jenny! Stop! It's Daddy!"

Toby, pale as the snow, stumbled forward. "Gosh, Dad! You *found* us! Jenny, you nearly *smothered* me." The remark brought Jenny quickly back to her senses.

"I did *not*!" she shouted angrily.

Skip grinned in relief. "I imagine your mother's ready to smother you both!"

"How'd you make 'em go away?" Toby asked eagerly.

Skip's face turned grim. "Let's forget it. You're safe now. Let's go."

At first, when Jenny and Toby saw their mother fling open the cabin door, they dreaded having to explain why they'd broken the one rule laid down by their parents — *don't go beyond the edge of the woods*.

But then she called out, "Skip! You've found them!" And even as she smothered them with hugs and kisses, the awful night in the forest was already turning into merely another adventure to add to their map.

"Now we're all going to sit right down and have some wonderful soup," Pat said, turning away from them.

Toby's eyes widened. "Aren't you even going to ask us what happened, Mom? Gosh! We had to build a snowhouse and —"

Pat turned back. Her face changed. She looked over at Skip. "Oh! It's so terrible," she cried. "Marybelle..."

Skip's face changed, too. "Marybelle! Pat, what happened?"

She covered her face and burst into tears. "It was my fault. I forgot to put Marybelle back. Oh, Skip! The wolf got her!"

"Marybelle!" Jenny and Toby both cried. "Oh, no!"

"I saw it happen," Pat shuddered. "It was a big, ugly black wolf!"

Toby whirled toward Skip. "Old Scarface?

Oh, Dad! You should have shot him! It's all my fault. If I hadn't just wanted to scare him off, Marybelle'd be OK this minute."

Skip put his arms around Pat. "Toby, we've had enough trouble for one family in twenty-four hours. Pat, honey, don't cry. Jenny, you and Toby get out of those clothes. Put the soup on the table. I'm hungry — and I'm *tired*."

But even though homecoming was not turning out to be a happy celebration, one happy fact stood out — nobody *blamed* anybody. The Robinsons were a family!

9

As though yesterday's storm had been clearing a path for springtime, the sun shone warm on Skip's back as he shoveled snow. He peeled off his jacket and flung it to the porch steps.

"Skip!" Pat looked out from the doorway. "What *are* you doing without your coat!"

Startled, he swung around. "Pat — what in the world is the matter with you? I'm shoveling snow. And I'm warm. Why?"

Without another word, she slammed the door shut. Skip stared for a puzzled second, then went on with the shoveling.

In the cabin, Jenny flipped off the radio.

"Can you believe it! *Another* storm on the way!"

Pat sighed. "Yes. I can believe it. What's hard to believe is that this winter will *ever* end."

Toby thumped down his spelling book. "I wish I was Samson," he said grumpily. "At least he can sleep all the time there's nothing to do."

He eyed the bear cubs snoozing over in the corner. Their peaceful, fat shapes gave him a wonderful idea. Draping himself in a blanket, he dropped on all fours. With a loud, roaring *grrr* he sneaked up behind the little bears. Results were great! The furry pair took off in a panic, Toby right at their heels.

"Toby! Stop!" Jenny yelled. "You're making a mess of everything."

Toby happily growled again and one cub made a frantic leap for the side table.

"Oh, no!" his mother screamed. "Stop!"

Too late! Over went the two-way radio, followed by the alarmed cub. He waddled quickly away from the disaster.

For a dreadful moment, there was utter silence as all three stared down. Their one link with civilization lay broken and useless.

Then Pat's voice rose higher and higher. "Toby! *You've ruined* the radio!"

"Mom, I'm sorry..."

"Sorry! What good will that do? You — you *broke* the radio!" She turned away and flung herself across the bed, sobbing wildly.

"Mom — Mom." Jenny reached out her hand. "Don't —"

Pat covered her ears and sobbed harder.

Shocked, Jenny stepped back. Then swiftly she ran to the door. Closing it softly behind her, she called, "Dad! Daddy! There's something terribly wrong with Mom. She's crying and crying."

Skip stared in dismay at the broken radio. "That's enough to make *me* cry," he said grimly. "What happened?"

Pat pushed up on one elbow. "Toby was playing. It was an accident. He didn't *mean* to —" Her voice broke and she began crying again.

"Kids," Skip said quietly. "Put on your things and go outside. I want to talk with your mother."

As the door closed behind the children, Pat sat up, still crying.

"Skip — I just couldn't take one more *thing*. When they're outdoors I never know what terrible thing is coming next. And the longer they're cooped up inside, the harder it is for all of us. Then *this* —" She waved a hand toward the radio. "We're completely cut off. And — and — I just don't *feel* good."

Slowly, the real truth came out. Pat Robinson had felt ill for weeks — ever since they'd come back from Three Forks. And she hadn't said one word about it!

Outdoors, Jenny and Toby began to feel the chill of rising wind. "The radio man said it would be a howler," Jenny said, shivering.

At the mention of the radio, tears began to stream down Toby's face. "I didn't mean to bust it," he said miserably.

Jenny's arm went around him. "I know that, Toby. It was an accident — just like Mom said."

Skip came out the door looking worried and upset. "Kids, your mother's sick."

"What's wrong, Daddy?" Jenny asked. "Does she have a temperature?"

"A little. But she doesn't have a cold or anything like that. I think Dr. Mike would say she needs a few days rest in bed."

"You coulda called him if I hadn't busted the radio," Toby said woefully. "It's my fault she's sick."

"Don't even think that, son. What she needs right now is knowing she doesn't have to worry about us. Just knowing winter's almost over is going to help, too. We're going to take good care of her."

"I wish she hadn't heard about the storm," Jenny sighed. "I guess that'll worry her."

"What storm?"

"The one we're going to have tonight. A real howler, was what the weatherman said."

Skip groaned. "Oh, fine! Well, we know what to do. Toby, you help me carry in more wood for the fireplace. Jenny, you see what you can figure out for lunch, will you?"

"And maybe we could fix the radio, Dad," Toby said hopefully.

Skip patted Toby's head. "Good idea."

By evening, in spite of patient work connecting broken wires, Skip and Toby failed to get the radio in working order. "We can receive but we can't transmit," Skip said gloomily.

Jenny gave him a warning glance. She said loudly and cheerfully, "It's a good thing we can hear all the news, isn't it?"

"Oh!" Skip glanced toward Pat who lay still and pale, her head turned away from them. "Sure is," he said. "Nothing like knowing what's going on."

The radio suddenly crackled. Mike McCord's voice came on. "Queen Roger Tango

Six Three Apple! Hello. This is Medic Two. Do you read me? What's going on up there? Come back.... Can you hear me? Over. Can you hear me? We've got a storm."

"That's not very newsy," Toby said. "Gosh, we can hardly see out the windows, they're drifted so high."

It was hard to keep spirits up. And the gale winds shrieking around the cabin and almost diving down the chimney did nothing to lighten the Robinsons' hearts. Even Crust moped around, looking dismal.

Skip stood up. "Toby, Jenny, you'd better go to bed. Let's all turn in."

Hardly were his words out than there was a terrible blast of wind, then a terrifying jolt on the back corner of the cabin roof.

Jenny screamed, and both children made a dive for the bed. Pat cried out weakly. "Skip! What was that?"

The bear cubs peeked out from beneath the bed and watched Skip investigate. Swirls of snowdust settled on his face as he looked up to inspect the damage. "Don't worry, Pat," he called over. "Probably just a limb from the tree at our back corner. Gosh! Sounded as though the cabin came down, didn't it?"

A tree branch! Only the whole tree's weight could have caused that fractured timber in the

roof. Quietly, and signaling Toby and Jenny to
say nothing, he went to the blanket storage
shelves. By standing on a chair, the hole in the
roof was in easy reach. Working as quickly as
he could, he wedged the blanket upward. At
least the cold and snow would be kept at bay
until proper repairs could be made.

In the morning, long before Jenny and Toby
were up, Skip was dressed and had a bright
fire going and a mug of tea made for Pat. He
had already shoveled a huge drift from the
cabin doorway.

He plumped up the pillows and helped her to
sit up. "Pat, honey — I've been figuring
what's best to do." He smiled and clasped her
hand. "Want to hear?"

She smiled faintly. "Sure!"

"Well, I don't think the medicines Mike left
with us are going to give you the help you
need. So — I'm going to go get him."

"Skip!" Pat sat up, nearly upsetting the tea
mug. "No! You can't make it. It's too far!"

Skip grinned. "What do you mean 'can't
make it'? Boomer makes it all the time and he
doesn't have skis. It's up and over the pass on
snowshoes. Then zip! Downhill all the way!"

Pat fell back on the pillows, tears falling.
"No."

Toby came sleepily down from the loft, rubbing his eyes. Jenny followed. They both saw the snowshoes, skis, rifle, and backpack stacked near the doorway. "Where you going, Dad?" Toby asked, suddenly wide awake.

"Going for help, Toby. I'll be depending on you to take care of things here. You, too, Jenny. Keep the soup kettle going!" Skip kissed each of them. "It's already clear as a bell outside, so don't worry about me. Keep the fire going and don't leave the cabin."

At the doorway he put on his snowshoes and swung up the rest of his gear. "Toby, I'm taking the rifle. I've left the shotgun." He paused. "You know how to use it, son."

Toby nodded. "Don't worry, Dad. I'll take good care of Mom."

"Crust — you stay," Skip said. "Stay, boy."

It was a winter wonderland beyond the open cabin door. Jenny and Toby waved anxious good-byes. Skip, waving back, struck out strongly across the white wilderness.

Far ahead above the timberline, blue sky dipped down to outline the pass. Snow sparkled along the long mountain range and Skip, plodding below in the fir forest, tried to choose the most direct pathway through the deep snow. Every shoving step ahead brought him nearer his goal and the sloping grade was growing steeper as he moved along.

Suddenly, a tremendous *crack* split the air, and then a long *rumble* loud as thunder. Terrified, Skip tried to look in every direction — the rumbling noise seemed to be all around him. And then, high up ahead, he saw a tumbling snow torrent pouring down, uprooting trees and boulders, rushing toward him like a fierce white Niagara.

With all of his strength he began awkwardly running through the fir trees, hoping to escape to the outer edges of the deadly winter trap.

For a moment, he thought he hadn't made it. Snow spray engulfed and blinded him. Then he realized he'd been tumbled over by the outside fringe of the avalanche. With a fierce effort he plowed his way out, clutching his rifle, and checking to see that the precious skis were not broken. Panting heavily, he stumbled to his feet and plunged on.

But hardly before he'd gone on a hundred feet a second roar filled the air. The awesome rumble shook the earth. Down came the tons of snow. And this time, Skip's luck almost ran out. Compared with the size of the avalanche, Skip felt as small and helpless as a snowflake. Still clutching the rifle, he lifted his arms, elbows bent, as though that could protect him from the mighty force rattling and pitching down the mountainside. For a moment, he felt himself scooped high. And the next thing he knew he was cartwheeling through the air — down, down, down.

In the cabin, the family heard the distant *booms*. Crust began to bark furiously and sniffed along the edge of the door. "You can't smell a boom, Crust," Jenny laughed.

"Well, he smells something," Toby said. He hesitated. "I'll let him look." Almost before the door was opened, Crust was out.

Toby screamed, "Crust!"

And no wonder. Close to the cabin, gaunt wolves stalked. Crust was on the attack! Grabbing the snowshovel by the door, Toby rushed into the very midst of the snarling, snapping pack, screaming at the top of his lungs.

"Toby! Come back!" Jenny yelled, horrified.

"What's wrong, Jenny?" Pat called weakly.

Toby grabbed Crust's collar and pulled him back to the door. Suddenly, in the fading light, a huge black wolf loomed up at the top of a snowdrift. Toby's face tightened in fear and shock. He jerked hard on Crust's collar, pulling him into the cabin. "Shut it!" he yelled at

Jenny. "Shut the door!"

White as a sheet, he leaned against the slammed door.

"Toby! What is it? What is it?"

"*Him*," Toby whispered. "*He's* out there. Old Scarface. I saw him!"

10

All through the dusk, Crust paced the cabin growling and sniffing at windows and the doorway. And as clearly as though they could really see them, Toby and Jenny knew the wolves were also sniffing, growling, and pacing on the other side of the snowdrifted cabin walls.

More for the sake of shutting out those sounds than for any real hope of news, Jenny turned on the radio. "Queen Roger Tango Six Three Apple. This is Medic Two. Come in, Skip."

Quickly, Jenny flipped the switch. "It's Dr. Mike. He's still trying to reach us." She shivered. "Gruesome," she muttered. Then walking over to her mother's bed, she spoke cheerfully. "Don't you worry, Mom. Nobody's forgotten us."

But Pat didn't turn her head. Eyes wide with fear, she lay staring into space. Jenny touched her. "Mom," she said gently. Pat didn't stir.

Uneasily, Jenny backed away. "Toby," she whispered, "I think Mom's *awfully* sick."

"What'll we do?" Toby asked, fright in his eyes.

Jenny had no answer, and wished she hadn't scared Toby. "Well, maybe we could get her to eat something. Why don't you build up the fire? It's not too warm in here. I'll fix us some burgers."

Almost as soon as the meat sizzled on the frying pan, a puff of cooking smoke rose up the stove vent. Overhead came a *thud*. Then another, and another.

Pat, white with fear, sat up. "They're up on top of the roof!" she screamed.

Jenny jerked the frying pan off the stove and set it aside. "It's the meat!" she gasped. "They've smelled the burgers! Oh, *Mom!*" she ran to Pat and threw her arms around her.

Toby, white-faced as his mother, lifted

Skip's shotgun off the wall. "Don't you worry, Mom. We're safe." He went to a window and scraped frost from it. "Can't see much out —"

His words broke off in a scream. A scarred, ugly-faced wolf, eyes glittering, glared back at him. "It's him! It's old Scarface!"

Crust bounded over, Jenny rushed up and grabbed him. "Get away from there, Crust! Don't smash the window!"

It took both Jenny and Toby to pull back the excited dog. They grabbed and hauled and pushed him. "Come on, Crust," Jenny begged. "We're all going to stay right by Mom."

Even the bear cubs scuttled over to the bed and hid beneath it. Only Bandido ignored the whole situation. He made himself comfortable by the fireplace and prepared for a good nap.

"You don't have to be scared, Mom," Toby said bravely after a few minutes. "They can walk around up there all they want to. We're in *here*!"

"And we're *safe*," Jenny said firmly. "See, Bandido knows it. He's asleep. I don't know why I yelled. It was silly."

"How about something else to eat?" Toby asked. "Jenny, why don't you make tea for Mom? Wolves probably don't like tea. And we could have — well, how about bread?"

"And jam." Jenny tried to smile and pretend those awful scraping noises on the roof simply weren't there. "Sure, Toby. And there's peanut butter, too. Why didn't I think of that in the first place!" She slid off the bed. "Mom, you just take a nap. I'll put the kettle on."

"I'll be right beside you," Toby said, patting his mother's hand.

Without speaking or looking at her anxious children, Pat closed her eyes.

It was while Jenny was making sandwiches that the awful fear-making thought struck her. "Toby!" she called softly. "Come here." Trying hard to sound very calm, and to keep her voice steady, she whispered. "Toby, we've got to stay awake all night. The blanket!"

Toby frowned. "What blanket?"

"The one Dad stuck in the roof. The wolves — " She swallowed and began again. "They might *pull it out*."

Dinner wasn't much of a success. Pat opened her eyes only long enough to wave a weak hand at the tea mug. "No, thank you," she murmured faintly. As for Jenny and Toby, it was hard to see the sandwiches when they could scarcely take their eyes off the wadded blanket in the back corner of the cabin roof.

But not until gray dawn was palely lighting

the cabin did disaster strike. Bandido, a good night's sleep behind him, went frisking about the cabin. He hopped up to a favorite shelf and scraped at the frosty pane. Just as Toby had been frightened, Bandido leaped back in terror. Green eyes glittered, white fangs showed, and a wolf smashed against the pane, breaking it.

Frantic, Bandido jumped from the shelf to the table. Over went the kerosene lamp. Up shot flames. Instantly, the calico curtains streaked fire.

"Jenny, Toby!" Pat lurched out of bed, screaming. "Get the water bucket!"

Nodding heads bobbed up. Jenny screamed. Toby ran for the water bucket. Pat staggered across the floor and came reeling back, broom in hand. Feebly, she swatted at the leaping flames. Jenny snatched a blanket and swung it with all her strength. But instead of smothering the flames it was turning into a lighted torch. Toby's try at flinging water only resulted in a huge splash running down the lower wall, and fire was reaching for the roof timbers and the wadded blanket.

Smoke was already fogging the cabin when flames, fed by the blanket, began to shoot up through the air space and spread across the shingles of the roof. A black column rose up to the dawn sky!

* * *

Only the thought of Pat, Jenny, and Toby kept Skip Robinson going. Ever since the avalanche had sent him tumbling over the canyon wall, he'd been dazed, bruised, aching — and frightened.

A night's sleep in a pine-bough shelter hadn't helped much. Stiff, half-frozen, he'd begun the long trudge up from the snow-filled canyon bottom. It was a miracle that he'd lost only his skis. Skip knew that fall could have meant his life. Wearily he plodded to the top of the ridge. "At least I have my rifle," he muttered. "The worst *must* be over. I should have — " He gasped. The worst was not over! Far down the mountainside, the cabin was in plain view. And to Skip Robinson's horror, a column of black smoke rose from the family roof!

Desperately, he lurched forward. "If only I had my skis! What's happened down there!"

Choking, coughing, half-blinded by stinging smoke, Jenny, Toby, and Pat kept up their losing fight.

Suddenly, there was a tremendous *plop*.

115

Squashing down onto the floor came a huge gush of snow.

Until the heavy smoke began pulling up through the hole in the roof, it was hard to believe the impossible had happened. "Mom!" Toby yelled. "The snow from the roof! It's put out the fire! It's OK!"

Pat looked up and Jenny cried out, "Mom!"

But Pat Robinson sagged, drooped, and, before the children could catch her, slumped to the floor.

"Mother!" they both screamed. Then, pulling and pushing, they managed to get her up and into bed.

"It's all over, Mom," Toby said. "Don't worry."

Tiredly, the two flopped down on the bed, watching the last curls of smoke lift up into the morning sky.

"Listen!" Jenny gasped.

Up above came a dreadful, familiar sound. Wolves — stalking the now exposed roof.

"It's them again," Toby whispered.

Crust moved beneath the hole in the roof, barking furiously. Suddenly he seemed to go mad. Leaping with all the power he had, he reached for the roof, snarling and snapping.

Frozen, the three watched. Into the opening, blotting out the morning sky, came old Scarface. His muzzle drew back above sharp fangs. His eyes glittered, green, wild, and blazing.

Pat screamed. "Toby! The gun!"

Once, Toby wouldn't let his father fire on old Scarface because the wolf was mad with hunger. Now, for the same reason, *he* would have to fire.

"Don't hit Crust!" Jenny screamed.

"Crust!" Toby yelled. *"Down!"* Pressing the heavy gun to his shoulder he took unsteady aim.

"Down, Crust!" Jenny yelled.

And Toby fired. In a tremendous explosion of blue smoke that sent him tumbling across the cabin floor, Toby faced what he'd had to do. Old Scarface was gone from sight!

But Crust set up a wild, furious barking. To Toby's horror, the ugly head pushed down from the hole again.

Toby reloaded and aimed once more. From outside came the sound of a sharp rifle crack. Then again and again shots rang out. "Daddy!" Toby yelled. "Dad's back!"

From the doorway Jenny and Toby saw the last of the fleeing wolves. And on the side hill of the cabin, their father, his hands cupped around his mouth, cried out, "Are you all right?"

"Daddy!" the children yelled joyfully. "Daddy!"

Skip, exhausted, struggled forward.

"Dad . . . I did it . . . I did it . . . I shot the gun!" Toby yelled.

Skip plodded up, hardly able to drag one foot after the other. "Kids! Kids!" He opened his arms wide. "How's mother?"

"She's — " Jenny began. "*Look*!"

A *chop-chop* sounded in the skies. A helicopter came over the pass. "It's Dr. Mike," Jenny yelled, bouncing up and down. "Everything's going to be all right now, Daddy!"

Coming straight down in front of the cabin, the 'copter threw a circling fan of snow. Out stepped Mike McCord, carrying his black bag.

"You're just in time! Mom's sick," Jenny called out.

Mike McCord shuffled through the drifts. "When I couldn't get you on the radio, I knew something was wrong," he said.

"You'll never know how glad I am to see you, Mike!" Skip held out his hand.

"Me, too," Toby beamed, throwing his arms around Mike.

"Anybody glad to see me?" a hearty voice called. Stan Coble stepped from the 'copter.

Not one of the Robinsons could have imagined just how much could have happened in the past twenty-four hours — or how much could happen now in just *one* hour.

Already, Stan had hammered down a temporary, but secure, repair on the cabin roof. Already, Skip, in fleecy slippers and warm bathrobe, was toasting his toes before Toby's fire. Already, Toby and Jenny had a stack of peanut butter and jam sandwiches ready for their company.

And best of all, Pat, propped up on pillows, was smiling at the whole world. Her cheeks were faintly pink and her eyes almost had their old sparkle. "Mike, I think you brought some kind of magic with you. I — I almost feel *good*."

Mike McCord laughed. "There's nothing you need that rest and mountain springtime won't cure. I'll run some tests, but it looks to me like a mild form of hypothermia combined with exhaustion and a bad case of TMW."

"What's that?" Toby asked. "Is it catching?"

Mike laughed. "Yep. It is. Lots of folks get it and live to tell the story. TMW stands for Too Much Winter."

Jenny called over, "The kettle's boiling. And I've got — "

There was a sudden loud stomping on the

cabin porch. Toby rushed to the door. "*Boomer!*" he cried joyously. Jenny flew behind him. "Boomer!"

Boomer slapped his floppy hat against his britches. "Wal, now! Wal, now. How-do ever'-body." He hugged both children and looked around quickly. "My goodness! Looks like a cyclone hit this place! Miss Pat, what's wrong? And Skip — what you doin' this time o' day arrayed in yore sleepin' gear?"

Stories poured out. Wolves. Avalanches. Fire. Old Scarface. Boomer lifted his hands. "I swear you outdone all I ever done in my life!" He looked sharply at Skip. "You get old Scarface?"

Skip shook his head. "Don't think so. He took off with the rest."

Boomer sighed. "Wal — pore old feller. Wouldn't be quite the same in these parts less'n he was a-patrollin' the wilderness." He paused. "Seems like bein' hungry ain't exactly his fault."

Pat shuddered. "Boomer, if you could have *seen* him!"

Boomer slipped an arm around Toby. "Glad I didn't. I'd shore a-had to take aim like Toby here."

Crust suddenly barked and rushed to the door, sniffing.

"He's back!" Pat cried, color draining from her face.

Toby paled. He hurried to the wall and took down the shotgun. Skip stopped him. "I'll handle it, son."

Snorting, grunting, whimpering sounds came from outside. Everybody but Boomer tensed. He sat back easily, eyes twinkling, as Skip flung open the door.

"Samson!" the children shouted.

Boomer grinned as Samson waddled forward, grunting with pleasure. The cubs and Bandido rushed to greet him. "Wal, you dadblamed, pesky, no-good bear! Yore back!" He looked over at Pat. "I'll be a horn-swoggled groundhog! Samson's no dummy. *Spring's a-comin'*. You hear me, Miss Pat? Spring's a-comin'!"

He walked over and bear-hugged Samson. "Right glad to see you...you old varmint!"

Spring! Even in the drifted snow, spring was out there, *somewhere*! And suddenly, it was a joyous world. Skip tossed Toby high in the air. Jenny flung her arms around Pat.

"We made it!" Skip shouted. "We made it!"

Dr. Mike grinned at Stan. "Looks like our wilderness family's OK, Stan."

Boomer haw-hawed. "*OK?* Doc, there ain't but two things this here family needs."

121

"Oh? What's that, Boomer?" Mike asked.

"Me," the old mountain man grinned. " — And a sight o' *sleep*. How about you comin' back another day?"

In the clear, beautiful light of noonday, the silvery helicopter lifted up.

"Bye!" Jenny, Toby, and Boomer shouted.

They waved and watched until the 'copter disappeared over the pass.

Jenny turned back to the porch steps. She paused and, bending down, brushed snow from the top of Pat's flower pot. "Toby! Boomer! Look!"

A pale, tiny green sprout peeked up from the snowy blanket.

Boomer grinned. "Told you. Samson's no fool." Holding each young Robinson close, he walked into the cabin. "Springtime," he called out, laughing. "You did it, Robinsons! You made it!"